BEADWORKS® 1998

LIGHT AND MYSTERY

by Kathlyn Moss

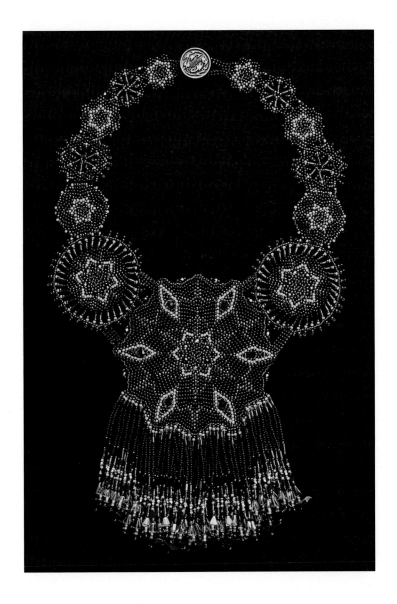

Autumn Arabesque by Kathlyn Moss, 7 x 13 x ⅜ in.; circular peyote-stitched rondelles with seed bead, vintage bugle bead, pressed glass crystal, amethyst, and horn bird fringe and vintage copper button closure. Photo by Dai Crisp.

CONTENTS

BEAD ART

BEAD ART

EDITED BY
ALICE KORACH

INTRODUCTION BY
KATHLYN MOSS

PHOTOGRAPHY BY
JIM FORBES

KALMBACH
BOOKS

© 1998 Kalmbach Publishing Company. All rights reserved. This book may not be reproduced in part or in whole without written permission of the publisher, except in the case of brief quotations used in reviews. Published by Kalmbach Publishing Co., 21027 Crossroads Circle, Waukesha, WI 53187.

Printed in Hong Kong

98 99 00 01 02 03 04 05 06   9 8 7 6 5 4 3 2 1

For more information, visit our website at http://www.kalmbach.com

Publisher's Cataloging in Publication
(Provided by Quality Books, Inc.)

Bead art / edited by Alice Korach ; introduction by Kathlyn Moss ; photography by Jim Forbes. — 1st ed.

p.   cm.
ISBN: 0-89024-367-0

1. Beadwork—North America. Beads. Korach, Alice.   II. Moss, Kathlyn, 1944–

NK3650.5.N6B43 1998   745.58'2'097
                              QBI98-32

Book design: Sabine Beaupré
Jacket design: Kristi Ludwig

Dust jacket photos: Front: *Mask* from *Let Me In/Let Me Out Family* by NanC Meinhardt (see pp. 62–65); Back: *Woman Who Runs with Poodles* by Laura Leonard (see pp. 56–57)

Great works of art have an element of mystery that cannot be fully explained.

—*Friedrich Nietzsche*

Beads are full of mystery; yet they are everywhere—from homes in the American Midwest to the halls of *haute couture* in Paris and Milan. Since time immemorial, they have beautified the objects of ritual, personal adornment, and fashion. Only now, at the end of the 20th century, have they found their place as a unique art medium. Today's artists have recast the material of the traditional past. Their fresh compositions, presented here in *Beadworks® 1998*, are signposts along the spiraling path of creative evolution.

Artists choose glass beads for their unique ability to transmit, reflect, and in some cases, absorb light—a property that so intensifies the color of a beaded work that it takes on the sparkling aura of the metaphysical. But beads are also actual objects that entice the artist to create unusual, highly tactile structures as well as vivid imagery—extravagance in concept, color, and composition naturally follows. "What other medium allows you to plunge your hands deep into boxes and sift beads through your fingers like gleaming grains of sand," declares artist Nancy Smeltzer. "I like the way light enters the beads, rolls around for a while on the inside, and then flies back out with a flash."

Many artists assemble thousands of individual beads into works of art; others make art by creating the bead itself. Seed beads, the principal material for beadwork, are used in much the same way as a painter uses dabs of pigment or a sculptor uses bits of clay. The nature of seed beads is unique, however, in that the artist can pick up only one tiny bead at a time, so the work progresses slowly. Often, artists find this process to be a form of meditation, rich with mystical significance. For NanC Meinhardt, "Art materials speak in a variety of tones with beads seeming to chant. Each bead is a tiny vessel of visual tone containing its own song to be bound together with others in a kaleidoscopic chorus of color suspended in light."

THE STAGE IS SET

Just a decade ago, two ground-breaking shows, *The Bead Goes On*, organized by Visual Arts Resources of the University of Oregon Art Museum, and *The Ubiquitous Bead*, curated by Ramona Solberg for the Bellevue Art Museum in Washington state, opened the eyes of many to the amazing possibilities of beads.

Exhibitions

The intervening decade has seen many more exhibitions. The most influential have been: *Surface and Structure: Beads in Contemporary American Art*, curated by Mark Richard Leach for the John Michael Kohler Arts Center, Sheboygan, Wisconsin, and the Renwick Gallery of the Smithsonian; *Pure Vision: American Bead Artists*, curated jointly by Sherry Leedy and B. J. Shigaki (a condensed show travels under the auspices of ExhibitsUSA, Kansas City, Missouri); *Contemporary Beads and Beadwork: Innovative Directions*, curated by Lynn Verschoor of the Loveland Museum/ Gallery of Loveland, Colorado; *Beadwork: Beyond Boundaries*, at Contemporary Artifacts Gallery in Berea, Kentucky; *The Beaded Object*, at the Folk Art Center, Asheville, North Carolina; *The Ubiquitous Bead: Tenth Anniversary Show*, Bellevue Art Museum, Bellevue, Washington; and *The Rebellious Bead*, curated by Leslie Campbell (touring under the sponsorship of Visual Arts Resources of the University of Oregon, Eugene).

Every year sees more events. The Dairy Barn Southeastern Ohio Cultural Arts Center in Athens, known for its *Annual Quilt National*, plans *Beadworks® 1998* as the first in a series of biennial exhibitions of beads and beadwork "that transcend their customary role as simple adornment or embellishment."

Organizations and conferences

The vitality of this new art form would not have been possible without the support of institutions like the many bead societies in the United States, Europe, and Japan. In addition to the original interest of members in bead history and collecting, many local bead societies—particularly those in Chicago; Minneapolis; Washington, D.C.; Los Angeles; Seattle; and Portland, Oregon—have provided a forum for disseminating information and instruction.

Starting with the International Bead Conference of 1990, programs specifically oriented to the interests of those creating beadwork and beads have become an important part of each gathering. This coming together of people from all over the world has had a significant impact on the growth of knowledge in all areas of bead history, materials, techniques, design, and inspiration.

While the International Bead Conference was the first to support this new art form, it is no longer the only one. *Embellishment*, sponsored by *BEAD& Button* magazine, and *Bead Expo*, produced by the Center for Bead Research and Recursos de Santa Fe and directed by Peter Francis, Jr., convene annually. Other conferences like *Convergence,* sponsored by the Handweavers Guild of America and the symposium of the Surface Design Association, while not oriented specifically toward beadwork, accept it as an art form within their purview. Recently, several new organizations and conferences have been established for artists making beads, including the Society of Glass Beadmakers and the National Polymer Clay Guild. These associations and conferences provide a place for artists, historians, vendors, and collectors to share information, sell their work, teach techniques, and interact with the public.

Teachers

Artist Joyce Scott, a favorite speaker at many conferences, has been and continues to be a pioneer in teaching bead-work. She has been spreading the word for nearly 20 years now. To aid in teaching, she wrote and illustrated *Fearless Beadwork*, a clever book that is as much about her irreverent take on life as it is about beadwork: "Trust yourself, there are few wrong turns in improvisational beadwork, just opportunities to get your 'but' in a sling. But the pursuit, adventure involved, is mesmerizing. These are little balls (I could make such a joke), so why worry!" Many artists credit Scott for showing them the way with beads—how to be fearless.

As people's desire to learn about beadwork has grown, more and more artists have begun teaching. Among the first to join Scott were Virginia Blakelock, Carol Perrenoud, Marcie Stone, and David K. Chatt. Blakelock wrote *Those Bad, Bad Beads*, a compendium of beadweaving techniques—both on and off the loom—including African and European techniques researched with Carol Perrenoud. Marcie Stone taught free-form peyote stitch, particularly as a vessel embellishment. As owner of the Shepherdess, a bead store in San Diego, she played an important role in disseminating information by bringing in many artists as instructors. David Chatt teaches a variety of off-loom techniques, particularly single-needle right-angle weave, which he developed after examining African beadwork. A new generation of teachers includes NanC Meinhardt, Carol Wilcox Wells, author of *Creative Beadweaving*, and Diane Fitzgerald, author of four books including *Sea Anemone Beadwork* and *Beads and Threads: A New Technique for Fiber Jewelry* with Helen Banes. Many others, too numerous to name here, instruct at

conferences, colleges, art centers, bead stores, and workshops. And often, each instructor has published a manual or book of techniques.

While a handful of people had been making beads from various materials for years, the arrival of a new material, polymer clay, and the revitalization of an old material, glass, ignited a whole new bead-making movement. Many of the artists who developed creative techniques for these media were soon teaching others. Harvey K. Littleton at the University of Wisconsin and Dale Chihuly, founder of Pilchuck Glass School near Seattle, were leaders in developing and teaching glass as an art form. And the first generation of glass beadmaking artist/teachers, including Brian Kerkvliet, Julie Clinton, Sage, Will Stokes, Don Schneider, and Donna Milliron, is still active. Many more continue their legacy of freely sharing information.

Nan Roche, author of *The New Clay*, was among the first to advocate the use of polymer clay for making art. Jamey Allen, Steve Ford, David Forlano, Tory Hughes, Pier Voulkos, Cynthia Toops, and Kathleen Dustin are among those artists who have developed and taught the creative potential of this new medium. All of the artists who teach say they love the experience, and all agree that the interaction with their students enriches their own work. Like proud parents, they are gratified when they see their students mature to create their own superb art.

With the recognition of beadwork and beadmaking as legitimate art forms, several schools and universities now include these techniques in their curriculum. Among the most prominent are Penland School of Crafts in North Carolina,

Arrowmont School of Arts and Crafts in Tennessee, Haystack Mountain School of Crafts in Maine, Oregon College of Arts and Crafts in Portland, and the University of Minnesota's Split Rock Arts Program in Minneapolis. It is now possible to receive an advanced degree in the study of beadwork and beads. Just 10 years ago, only Joanne Laessig had found a way to do it at Northern Illinois University.

Publications

Books and magazines have also played a key role in inspiring and teaching many. Not long ago, the publications dealing with beads and beadwork could be counted on one hand; but, happily, the last decade has seen an outpouring of writing on the subject. Most influential have been *The History of Beads* by Lois Sherr Dubin, *Collectible Beads: A Universal Aesthetic* by Robert K. Liu, and *The New Beadwork* by Kathlyn Moss and Alice Scherer, which opened thousands of eyes to the creative promise of beads.

For nearly 20 years *Ornament* was the only magazine that focused on beads as an art form. Since the late 1980s, *FiberArts*, *Threads*, and *American Craft* have included many articles about beadwork and beadmaking, and *Lapidary Journal* began to publish an annual issue dedicated to the subject. Magazines like *ARTnews* and *Art in America* have reported on the beadwork of Sherry Markovitz, Joyce Scott, and Liza Lou. 1994 saw the introduction of *BEAD& Button*, a magazine committed to providing quality instructional material and profiling beadworkers and beadmakers.

Artists are not only writing how-to books, but using the current recording technology to produce instructional videos. Virginia Blakelock and Carol Perrenoud were among the first with *Bead Woven Necklaces* and *Beadweaving: Peyote Stitch*. Computers are also important tools—from aiding in design, to communication, to running glass furnaces. Perhaps the most striking technological innovation in the last five years is the Internet, linking publishers, universities, organizations, and suppliers. Even individual artists now have web sites.

Bead availability

The last ten years has seen a huge increase in the use of beads by the general public. All this enthusiasm has generated phenomenal growth in the number of bead stores. Beads can now be found in mall stores, crafts stores, and antiques stores, as well as sewing and quilting shops. Manufacturers in the Czech Republic, Austria, France, India, and Japan have greatly increased their production of beads, adding more colors, finishes, and designs. All this growth has been a real boon to artists, who now have access to a wider variety of beads and supplies than ever before. Finally, everything is in place for them to create the works of their dreams.

BEADWORK AT THE END OF THE 20TH CENTURY

The dream pieces in *Beadworks® 1998* articulate a maturity in aesthetic content and the emergence of several thematic directions. While most of the works here are physically small, their emotional effect is large. Bead art is not about mere cerebral exercise, but about capturing the intense sensory stimulus present in the glittering light of beads. It elevates an object above the ordinary—to the sublime. Not for the faint of heart, the pieces in *Beadworks® 1998* are power objects, containing and radiating the energy condensed into their making.

The notable themes of this decade are realized within the three-dimensional narrative of the human body, the harmonies of nature, the strange juxtapositions of surrealism, and the coolness of abstract geometry. An artist's cultural heritage, gender, or sexuality can also be a significant resource for creative expression. Still others have discovered the best material within their own lives.

Interior reality

For Joan Dulla, being the survivor of incest has guided the focus of recent works like *Don't Tell—If you tell, it will Kill your Mother* and *That's How it Looks to a Little Kid*. "Certainly my history has been a huge influence," she explains, "my jewelry has gone from being pretty, cute, and funny stuff to statement work that isn't much fun to look at and sometimes brings tears and sadness."

Mimi Holmes and Dustin J. Wedekind use the beauty of beadwork to make the perplexing and discomfiting issues of sex and desire approachable. Holmes' *Weighted with Desire* is one of a series of mixed-media sculptures through which she has spent years exploring her fears, desires, and relationships. At first glance, her work might be mistaken for an insect or a seedpod, but it always refers to the human body and being female. While Holmes' allusions can be oblique, Wedekind's imagery in *Blue Glass* and *Twelve Bulge* is direct. "Beads are sexy. I use the seductive nature of the beads to draw the viewer into these sexual representations," explains the artist. "I want to address sexual identity, to find meaning and beauty in the human form."

The human body

For other artists, the human body is the template upon which they build concepts of color, texture, and story. Ann Terepaugh Mitchell, creator of *Dumbbell* and *Refugees*, studied art anatomy in Madrid and approaches the figure and its forms from a classical perspective. Equally, she is fascinated by the twinkling, impressionistic light inherent in glass beads. She considers this vibrant luminosity as important as the sculpted form. Although many of the same attributes exist in *Hot Line* by Valorie Harlow, presenting a recognizable experience is most important to her. She wants the viewer to feel the pull of a familiar emotional connection.

In *Fable Vessel* and *Hiding in her Mother's Skirts*, NanC Meinhardt raises the personal story to the level of myth when she deliberately entangles numerous figures within a densely layered, claustrophobic structure. Layered texture, more than anthropomorphic form, is the key to understanding *Getting Ready*, *Sabotaging the Working Woman*, and *Sloth Girl* by Michelle Williams. Both artists produce copiously beaded structures of striking visual intensity—an intensity that is enhanced by, yet does not depend upon, a particular palette to achieve its impact.

Using peyote stitch and primary colors, Patty Haberman, Laura Leonard, and Liz Manfredini bring humor and that magical familiar, the animal, to their work. For Haberman it's fish. *Swimming with the Big Fish* is a witty take on how to reduce stress and regain control: "Quit worrying and just take the 'plunge'—dive in and swim with the fish!" One can't help but think of all those fish tanks in dentists' offices. In *Woman Who Runs with Poodles*, a parody on the book by Clarissa Pinkola Estes, Leonard pokes fun at the mystical to celebrate the mundane. And what is more ordinary than that Fifties symbol, the poodle.

Liz Manfredini, by substituting a cow for a horse in *The Dairy Queen*, champions a unique take on the legend of Lady Godiva and America's love affair with ice cream. While recognizable imagery is important to these artists, each feels more attached to the meditative process of beading. "Because of the time involved, I can't remember exactly what I did in making a piece," muses Leonard, "so it's magical when it's done."

In *She Again* and *Spin*, Sally Wassink weaves a depiction of the mythic woman as the embodiment of "the creative spark, its connection to the divine, and the belief that it exists in everyone."

Dolls are perhaps the most magical manifestation of the human form. Usually they are considered mere toys, but sometimes, as in art and ritual, they have deeper meanings—as stand-ins for people and as repositories of myth. "My dolls, like *Auburn Beauty*, *If I Were Going*, and *Murtha Bacon Salmo*, are 3-D characters in stories," says Christy Puetz. "I use distorted, but still recognizable figures, which I make by sewing jewel-toned beads over black fabric. Like quilts, my dolls contain special items that I've collected. I never use bright colors, and I think pink is absolutely 'evil.' I want to stir up people's memories and ideas when they see the dolls. People always bring

personal baggage to the experience." Talismanic power also resides in the beaded fibrous body of *Little Bit* by Olga Dvigoubsky Cinnamon. "As an artist, I seek to fashion relationships by creating pieces that insist people interact with them, explore their profusion of color and diverse textures."

The head

For Carolyn Veerjee, Ann Terepaugh Mitchell, and NanC Meinhardt, just the face or head can convey as much visual energy as a full figure. The nubby visage of *Ardent* by Carolyn Veerjee presents a powerful presence, the result of combining an ancient technique, beadwork, with a modern one, electroforming (a type of metal plating most unusual in this medium). In *The Perm*, Mitchell creates the bust of a conventional woman undergoing a peculiar transformation through the excessive buildup of textures and forms in somewhat repellent colors. The portraits in Meinhardt's *Let Me In/Let Me Out Family*, with their complexly decorated features, allude to the historical uses of masks that both hide and reveal the psychological elements of human relationships. Portraiture that communicates relationships and character is also fundamental to understanding *Three of the Brothers* by Rosie Dixon and *The Pileated* by Lisa Lew.

The torso

While the head holds meaning for some artists, the classical torso form intrigues others. *Family Tree* by Susan Fraerman employs beads in rich autumn colors to portray her feelings about the grandmother who "died too young, leaving behind unanswered questions, but who also left a legacy of joy in creating with needle and thread." For Jacqui B. Fehl, *The Bride*, collaged with painstakingly glued-on pictures and beads, is an extravagant statement about the convoluted relationship between a woman and a man—with the snake, among other symbols, making a pointed reference to Eve. *The Three Furies* is composed of three body forms, each wearing an elaborately beaded and decorated velvet bustier, a garment with armor-like overtones. The sculpture, created in collaboration by Diane Fitzgerald, Valorie Harlow, and Barbara McLean, points to woman's role as moral arbiter. Before *Untitled Jacket*, Robert Burningham's work resembled colorful paintings of elaborately stitched and beaded designs. Like paintings, these pieces were stretched flat and framed. The rounded, sculptural torso form implied by the jacket is a breakthrough for him.

Jewelry

In the medium of beads, jewelry is the ultimate interactive art form. Jewelry, especially the necklace, can be more than classic adornment. It can manifest the power of myth and still be wearable. In JoAnn Feher's *Garden Party*, the fully sculpted beaded figures of two women and a devilish satyr put a humorous spin on the serious story of sin and guilt. Debra Dembowski is more interested in portraying the sacred aspect of woman in *Female Icon with Wings*, *Love Goddess*, and *Upside Down Woman*. Primarily a silversmith, she uses beads in fringe and mosaics to bring the opulence of color and the sensuality of touch to her work.

For Jocelyn Giles, the journey of creation is as important as the finished piece. "The trick is to keep the possibilities open during the creative process," she says. "In *Pollen Chain*, I was able to let the piece go where it needed to, I didn't place demands on it, such as making it turn out pretty." *Blue Gallé, Green Moss* by Sandy Swirnoff explores the properties of glass, both as an object and as a textile woven from beads. In *Colette* and *Zazou*, Kathryn Harris employs the rarely-used technique of wiring beads. This technique bestows both a stiffness and a flexibility to her neckpieces and makes possible unique structures and interlacings.

Bead embellishment

While most beadwork is assembled with needle and thread and may be viewed as a fiber art, beads, not thread, should be the elemental medium—the imagery should be composed of and dependent upon beads. Thus, although the fiber pieces by Pamela Schloff, Amy Orr, Beth Barron, and Rachel Roggel contain beads, they are not beadwork. That said, the beads in their pieces still function as more than embellishment. Beads bring texture and light to these compositions in a way that no other medium can. They create an exhilaration that transcends the physicality of the materials and suggests the spiritual. "In *Midwest Mecca*, beads add the unique qualities of smallness of color and glint. The small bits of color invite the viewer to come closer," Schloff notes, "and the glint adds a subtle design element that causes an illusion of movement." *Row House #14* and *Row House #15* by Amy Orr are from a series of works fabricated from the castoffs of urban society. They represent her reflections on community. "In these two row houses, elegant glass beads contrast with the unexpected—lead pellets and shot up aluminum," comments Orr. "My work has always been about contrast and impact and about making art from the senseless."

Beth Barron's *Of Lace, Hankies, and Tears* depicts a story that begins with photo-transfers of herself as a child, her father, and her grandmother. These pictures are surrounded by silvery beads stitched onto her grandmother's hankies, which Beth ripped up and reassembled. "Beads bring sparkle, but have sharp edges, a metaphor for the joy you find in the sadness of life. As a girl, I used to open the drawers of my grandma's dresser," remembers Barron, "to look at the tumble of things inside. Some of these old things got used in this piece about love, family secrets, and innocence lost. 'Tears' can be read two ways—tears from women like my grandma crying into these absurdly delicate hankies, and me tearing them up." Rachel Roggel also finds imagery in her family and culture. She uses buttons like two-holed beads. Sometimes she applies them in dense layers as in *Dust into Gold*; more often she sews them into patterns like the beautiful spiral maze in *The Road to Jerusalem*.

Abstraction

Not all of the pieces in *Beadworks® 1998* are figurative. Nancy Smeltzer, Laura Willits, Richard LeMieux, and Betty Pan find inspiration in abstraction and geometric forms. In *Jungle Garden* Smeltzer abstracts flowers and leaves into heavily beaded swirls of hot color. For Laura Willits, it's the cool distillations of the midnight hour that are woven into *Eclipse* and *Span I*. Richard LeMieux's two works titled *Cross* are distillations of

another kind—the luminous geometry of symbol. LeMieux uses the cross, a contradictory emblem of both coming together and pulling apart, to explore a "very loaded image outside of cultural conditioning." In *Kaleidoscope*, Betty Pan revels in the pure geometry innate to the grid of beadwork.

The container

Recently David Chatt has become fascinated by the concept of interactivity, where one is required to handle the various components of a work in order to appreciate the sculpture fully. While *Puzzle Box* is about one shape being unfolded to create others, *Toy Box* is a container of miniature working models.

Many artists use the container or vessel to explore the sculptural and symbolic concepts of emptiness and fullness. "The graphic quality of *Millennium Celebration Goblet* was inspired by Art Deco patterns and the bright colors of Japanese kimono," says Madelyn Ricks. "The form refers to the ritual cups used in African religions." Covered in colorful circles, Terry Bell's beaded jar, *Circles of Life*, serves as an allusion to the comforts of quilts, canning, and nourishment, and contains significant aspects of her friend's life. *Bean Pot* by Alison F. Whittemore demonstrates the artist's ability to find creative nourishment by transforming discarded objects. Colleen O'Rourke's *Darkness*, an apparently empty vessel, wears its metaphors on its surface, bearing the image of a lone woman in the landscape of night. The wildly textured surface and staring yellow-bead eyes of *Gorgon Medusa* by Lisa Niforos embody her concept of woman as a mythic force of nature.

Nature

The strong, yet ephemeral, forms of nature carry meaning for many artists who create with beads. They see beads as being like tiny stones or cells that fit elegantly together to construct the whole. For several years, Chris Allen-Wickler has been developing a series of mystical earthworks, including *Visible Soul: Eight Year Elegy*, *Visible Soul: Jule's Journey*, and *Visible Soul: Zoë's Imagination*, that express deep spiritual values. "I encase well-worn riverbed rocks in taunt, shiny skins of beadwork with fingerholes just large enough to touch the rock (soul) within," says Allen-Wickler. Her poem, "Prayer for our Earth" explains the elemental power of beads:

Give us our bodily envelope, the momentary shelter of elements that have belonged to a whirl of bees, whispering leaves, and the warm breath of the million deaths recorded in every inch of built rock and dense memories.

Give us heightened feeling for the organic rhythm of all things, to be united with the trembling and flow of our green blood. Let the wind slide over the waves, patting them with its giant hand and the sea stretch its muscles in the deep. Liquid singing.

Give us the larger picture, the longer view, faith in our own epoch. Give us the fire to see against the darkness, as a plume of sparks rises and flies at our ripe hearts like startled birds. Standing on the crest of the light between fixity and vertigo, you are the diaphanous balance.

Nancy Eha's *In the Garden of Beadin'* takes a more whimsical look at the beauty of nature and beads as having the power to engulf the unwary. She skillfully uses the lush reds and greens of plants to balance the shooting firecracker dynamic of the floral shapes. With the same red and green colors, the jewel-like *Michigan Apples* by Barb Davis depicts a more peaceful view of nature.

Surrealism

A few artists find creative energy in the unnatural and dreamlike associations of surrealism. The disconcerting imagery of hard beads as soft and draping in *How to Separate an Egg* and *Pasta Again* by Eleanor Lux brings to mind that icon of surrealism, *Object: Cup* by Meret Oppenheim. Nicole Nagel, John Lefelhocz, and JoAnn Baumann are intrigued by the edginess of beadwork created from non-bead materials. Nagel's *Soaked*, a vessel woven with cubes of sponge, is a bucket that both will and will not hold water. "A mundane object, altered and reevaluated, has the potential to become an object of intrigue," asserts the artist. For John Lefelhocz, intrigue resides in the subtle changes of pattern that occur with repetition. To pursue these subtleties, he created *One Month, One Week, and One Day* by stringing brightly painted bicycle wheel parts on a steel rod like a strand of mad beads on bent wire. Mundane thread bobbins are the "beads" of *All Strung Out, AKA Menopausal Mama* by JoAnn Baumann, a sculpture that is both ancestral figure and self-portrait.

Handmade beads

With its beadlike masks nestled in a matrix of free-form peyote stitch, Jan Nix-Westhoff's collar *Masquerade* connects beadwork and beadmaking. She sculpted the many personages of the mask beads from polymer clay. Carol Shelton also used polymer clay in a complex process of stacking, cutting, and thinning to make the shaded beads in *Desert Dust Devils*. "I like to watch as the colors are pushed together and change gradually, leaving a trail of their origins," she explains. "I cut narrow strips from the clay slab and wound them around each bead to create spirals. I especially like the spiral form because it is dynamic."

Ken Arthur carved deer bone to create the ribs of *Katie's Breastpiece*, a ritual necklace assembled with hair and shell that draws its form and inspiration from Native American culture. In *Inspired By Iolite* Thalia Tringo flameworked three layers of glass into luminescent purple-blue beads. She strung these with gold beads to create a necklace reminiscent of classical Roman jewelry. Kristen Frantzen Orr also flameworks glass into beads. But, unlike Tringo's emphasis on pure color, Orr's beads contain bits of encased gold foil and frits (powdered glass). Thus, the beads for *Seen in a Telescope* seem to sparkle with stars like the night sky, and the beads for *Seen in the Dishpan* capture the sheen of oil on water. Inspired by her copper scouring pad, she also crocheted copper wire into beads. *Hanger's Delight* by Sylvia deMurias is the result of artistic recycling. "I used coat hangers to make the links for the necklace and cobalt blue glass bottles for the beads," she reveals, "I feel gratified when I am able to transform ordinary, discarded materials into lovely wearable art."

Finally, with the colorful, highly textured beaded beads of Ruth Marie Satterlee, the journey from beads to beadwork has come full circle. The medium is the artifact, and the artifact is the medium in its purest sense.

THE ARTISTS

Chris Allen-Wickler

Visible Soul is a body of work consisting of river rocks covered in peyote stitch. Chris begins with the stone as a metaphor for the soul, imagining both as solid, worn, and eternal with the capacity to rise from the core while still remaining gravity-bound. The process of stitching beads, the fragile "skin" of the soul, is "labor intensive and lingering. It is a way of making a mark and becomes a remnant of the passage of time, a memory of breath, a record of pulse, an accumulation of wisdom and authority." The windows in the beadwork show the soul in glimpses that make the viewer search for the potential hidden within.

Chris has been working with beads for eight years and is also known for her large-scale environmental textiles. A graduate of Cranbrook Academy of Art, she credits Joyce Scott with bringing her to beadwork. She spends two to three months on each piece and gains the greatest pleasure from the meditative aspect of beadwork.

Visible Soul: Eight Year Elegy
6 x 5 x 4 in.; seed beads, thread,
and river rock; using peyote stitch
(far left)

Visible Soul: Zoë's Imagination
7 x 5 x 5 in.; seed beads, thread,
and river rock; using peyote stitch
(bottom)

Visible Soul: Jule's Journey
9 x 6 x 4 in.; seed beads, thread,
and river rock; using peyote
stitch (top)

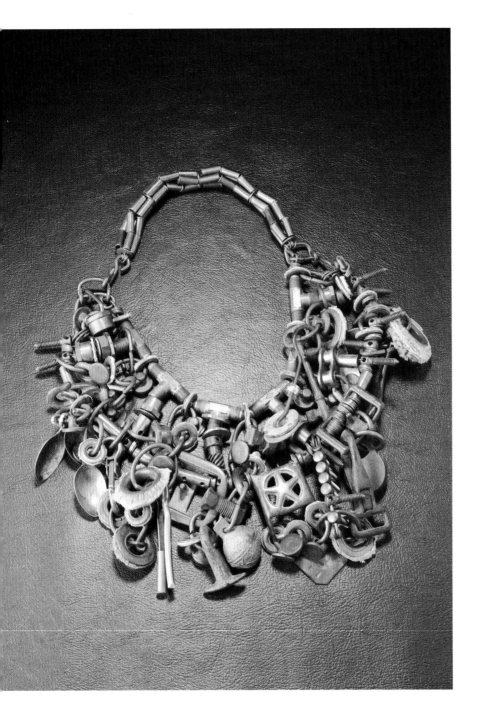

Kenneth A. Arthur

Ken makes and uses "beads" that challenge common assumptions about the nature of beads. Art is his way of life and his living. In addition to using beads for 10 years, he carves wood and stone, sculpts, and welds in a reconstructed barn-studio. He created the necklace, *My Dad's Drawer*, as a tribute to his handyman father, who kept everything because "it might be needed someday." *Katie's Breast Piece* was inspired by the patterns of many indigenous cultures. It is accented with its owner's hair and is intended to be worn for special occasions, ceremonies, and rites of passage.

My Dad's Drawer
11 x 14 x 2 in.; necklace of brass shells, plumbing parts, electrical fittings, grommets, gears, links, spoons, locks, washers, and buckles; assembled on a wire frame and filled in with rings

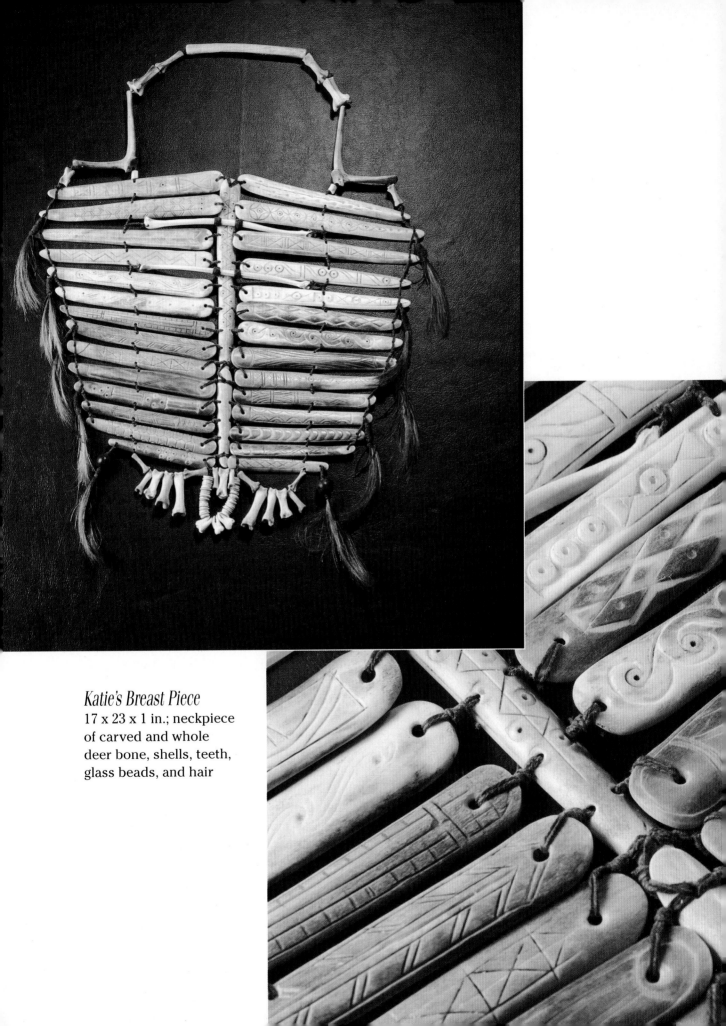

Katie's Breast Piece
17 x 23 x 1 in.; neckpiece
of carved and whole
deer bone, shells, teeth,
glass beads, and hair

Beth Barron

Beth became a fiber artist 20 years ago as a weaver but was captivated by fabric. Quilting and embroidery led her to beads about two years ago. According to her, "Beads sparkle and are reflective, a quality I seek in others, in life, and in myself. They are substantial when joined together." She often works on more than one piece at a time and is drawn to the meditative act of sewing beads to a surface one by one.

She strives to learn about herself as she works and is particularly inspired by other female artists. For her, handwork has meaning and restores balance to her life, helping her to bring order to chaos and fragmentation. Starting an exploration of loss, Barron used her grandmother's hankies and lace for *Of Lace, Hankies, and Tears*. She was struck by their delicacy in contrast to their intended purpose, absorbing the tears and pain of women, and felt compelled to tear them as a symbol of grief.

Of Lace, Hankies, and Tears
15 x 16 in.; beads, lace, hankies, silk flowers, buttons, photo transfer, and embroidery thread; joined with hand embroidery

JoAnn Baumann

JoAnn says that when she began beading about five years ago, "it just felt right." She now beads 60 to 70 hours a week. For her, weaving intricate patterns with the tiny detail that beads allow is meditative and magical. She particularly enjoys the continuing dialog between herself and the piece.

She worked on *All Strung Out, AKA Menopausal Mama* for 80 hours, driven and doing nothing else until it was finished. She created it to help her connect with her mother and grandmother at the scary menopausal period of her life. The thread bobbin beads recall her grandmother, who was a milliner as a young girl. Strips of fabric used as the color in the piece come from her mother's silk blouses. She is the figure, which like her, is woven from the fabric of her ancestors.

All Strung Out,
AKA Menopausal Mama
10 x 21 x 8 in.; seed beads, Nymo thread bobbins for beads, and silk blouse fabric strips worked between rows of brick stitch

Circles of Life
9½ x 4–in. diam.; Glass jar
and lid covered in seed
beads with peyote stitch;
contains 50 etched mir-
rors framed in seed bead
netting

Terry Bell

Terry has been using beads for over 40 years, but she has done only woven beadwork for the past two years, working at it full time. She feels that as the maker, she is the primary beneficiary of her work because while weaving she travels on an introspective journey that bonds her mind and the medium. She says, "Beadwork soothes my senses and allows my inner voice to come out as little bits of dancing light." She loves both graphing and beading and asks, "How can something so small and unassuming be so sensual?"

Circles of Life celebrates the 50th birthday of a dear friend of 35 years. To Terry, the circle symbolizes the never-ending energy of the human spirit. Here it also represents all the important people in her friend's life. Inside are 50 beaded, round mirrors with etched words reflecting her memories.

Robert Burningham

Robert has been beading since 1970. A retired dentist, he spends about two years, working 40-60 hours a week, on each piece. Originally, his work was primarily embroidery with some beads; now it's mostly beads with some embroidery. For him, the pleasure of using beads, the way they are highly influenced by the constantly changing light, is also the greatest challenge. As he works the light constantly fluctuates. Thus, only when he completes a piece is he able to enjoy the interaction of texture, color, and design. He credits Walter Nottingham, Constance Howard, Joyce Scott, and the process of working and maturing in his medium with having the most influence on his work. He has recently branched out into lampworking.

Beaded and Embroidered Jacket
22 x 21 in.; beading: many sizes and kinds of beads, mostly seed and Japanese cylinder beads, some small porcelain beads; beads hand-sewn separately or sewn six at a time and couched between each; embroidery: silk, linen, rayon, and cotton threads, metallic gold thread couched to define outer edges of design elements; jacket constructed by Charlene Burningham

David K. Chatt

David is an innovator who loves the process of discovery. He says, "When I figure out how and know that it came from my head, my heart, and my hands, it is extremely rewarding." He has been beading for 11 years and spends 400 to 500 hours on a piece, working at it full time when he's not traveling or teaching.

All his recent work explores the techniques of self-supported bead sculpture. *Puzzle Box* offers the viewer a tactile experience. The puzzle pieces must be taken from their compartments and the puzzle assembled. Since it is two-sided, when the pieces are replaced the geometric designs on their surfaces can be arranged many ways. *Toy Box: A Sampler* is another interactive sculpture. One cannot fully appreciate the pieces without handling them and exploring the secrets concealed in each. Each of the nine pieces represents a technical discovery.

David comments that although beads have been part of so many cultures for so many centuries, it is only recently that we have started to explore the possibilities fully. "There is something very rewarding about being on the front lines as this medium goes from the kitchen table to some of the finest galleries, museums, and collections in the world. In my work, I endeavor to push the boundaries of what we traditionally think of as beadwork. I want to do the unexpected, the best of which I am capable."

Puzzle Box
6 x 6 x 2 in.; 11/0 seed beads and thread; worked in right-angle weave (above)

Toy Box: A Sampler
7 x 7 x 4 in.; a silk-upholstered box contains toys that also contain toys, all constructed of 11/0 seed beads and thread; worked in right-angle weave (right). Photos by Larry Stessin

Olga Dvigoubsky Cinnamon

Olga has been involved in fiber art for about 30 years, having grown up in a household of skilled handworkers. She has been making figurative crocheted, stuffed sculptures for seven years and beading them extensively for five. Her favorite beads are asymmetrical, and she most enjoys selecting the bead colors and textures with which to clothe her figures.

For Olga, the end result takes second place to enjoying the creative process. Each figure is an attempt to fashion a relationship with the viewer. The profusion of color and the feeling of different textures insists that the viewer interact with the work. She credits Joyce Scott and her sense of humor for involving her in beadwork.

Little Bit
5 x 8 x 1½ in.; crocheted with waxed linen, cotton, and metallic threads; glass and metal bead embellishment and cotton fabric stuffing

Barb Davis

Barb says the reason for her bead obsession is that she didn't finish her beading in a past life. She's working hard—about 80 hours a week—to make up the deficit. She has been beading for about 12 years and spends about six months on each piece. Her favorite hobby is buying beads.

Michigan Apples
9 x 9 x 9 in.; 15/0
seed beads and wire
wrapping; apples are
handmade vintage
glass shank buttons

Debra Dembowski

Debra was painting and drawing in 1988 when she attended *Structure and Surface, Beads in Contemporary Art* at the Michael Kohler Arts Center in Sheboygan, Wisconsin. She was so amazed that she had to go back for a second look. In 1989 she began working in metal, adding beadwork five years later because she felt the need for color.

Her complex pieces combine silversmithing and metalwork, stone carving, and seed bead work. She enjoys the loud power equipment and aggressive pounding and filing of the first two activities and finds the beadwork a welcome retreat. After carving the face from marble, pipestone, or ivory nut, she sews branched fringe around the head for stylized hair. Finding ways to connect the beadwork without compromising the strength of the whole is always a challenge. She also creates micro-mosaics by placing tiny seed beads one by one into a silver bezel body on two-part epoxy with tweezers. She fills the mosaic with a specially formulated hard wax. Many pieces also include a carved stone base so they can both adorn the wearer and also enrich the environment where they reside.

Love Goddess
2 x 4¾ x ½ in.; 12/0 cylindrical seed bead branched fringe hair, hand carved and stained marble face, micro-mosaic heart body of tiny 3-cut seed beads, and carved alabaster heart stand (above)

Female Icon with Wings
2½ x 3½ x ½ in.; 14/0 seed bead branched fringe hair, hand carved ivory nut face, micro-mosaic wings of tiny 3-cut seed beads, petrified palm wood, picasso stone, and vintage beads

Upside Down Woman

3½ x 6 x ½ in.; 14/0 seed bead branched fringe hair, carved and stained marble face, sterling silver articulated body, vintage bead necklace

Hanger's Delight—A Necklace of Links
15–in.–long necklace; handmade links from rusted steel coat hangers and lampworked bottle glass

Sylvia deMurias

Sylvia says, "I collect things, many things." She is interested in both the concept and the reality of recycling, so *Hanger's Delight—A Necklace of Links* is made from recycled, rusted steel coat hangers and cobalt-blue glass bottles lampworked into beads. It gives her great pleasure to be able to transform ordinary, discarded materials into wearable art. Other pieces incorporate drilled beach stones and glass. Sylvia has been working in metal for about 15 years and has been lampworking for five.

Rosie Dixon

Rosie inherited beads from her grandmother, so in her quest to sort out the whos and whys of her family, beading a family portrait just seemed to fit. She has been working in bead embroidery for the past four years, using the techniques of Zen beadwork, which she learned from Carol Berry, and needlepoint adapted from *Oriental Carpets in Miniature* by Frank Cooper. She says she loves using beads. She gathers a palette and then uses whatever hops onto her needle, saying, "It always works."

Three of the Brothers is part of Rosie's family portrait. The three brothers are shown as acrobats standing on their heads for the father. The beading is tight and cramped to symbolize their turmoil and confusion, in contrast to the Oriental carpet frames that are a metaphor for the appearance of respectability and affluence of families in the '30s and '40s. Each brother lives in his own box, isolated from the others, yet locked together just the same.

Joan Dulla

A metalsmith for 10 years, Joan added beads and beadwork about five years ago to satisfy her hunger for color. She also enjoys the contrasting activities of forging and fabricating metal and meditatively stitching tiny seed beads.

That's How it Looks to a Little Kid, she says, took her a lifetime to create. "It floated around in my head for years until I finally got up enough courage to make it." She spent two months fabricating it and another beading and could only work on it while her children were at school; she hid it when they returned. "It was the hardest piece I ever made." *Don't Tell—If you tell it will Kill your Mother* is a necklace made of a gasket clamp with a narrow loom-woven strip of black and white beads that says "don't tell, don't tell, don't tell," spiraling around the inside. The words, "If you tell it will Kill your Mother," spiral around the outside. As the clamp tightens, it gets smaller to shut off leaks. Telling has become Joan's artistic mission.

Don't Tell – If you tell it will Kill your Mother
5 x 5 x 1 in.; necklace loom beaded with 14/0 seed beads, silver-colored gasket clamp

Three of the Brothers
40 x 10 x 2½ in.; seed bead embroidery (left)

My work is my history.
I am an incest survivor.
It is about
agony,
terror,
pleasure,
shame,
tears,
pain,
suffering,
envy,
indignity,
blame,
betrayal,
happiness,
invasion,
humiliation,
horror,
fear,
favorites,
secrets,
terror,
horror,
vomiting,
weeping,
heaving,
hiding,
confrontation
denial,
exposure,
pain,
suffering
forgiveness
calmness
closure.

But I never will forget.

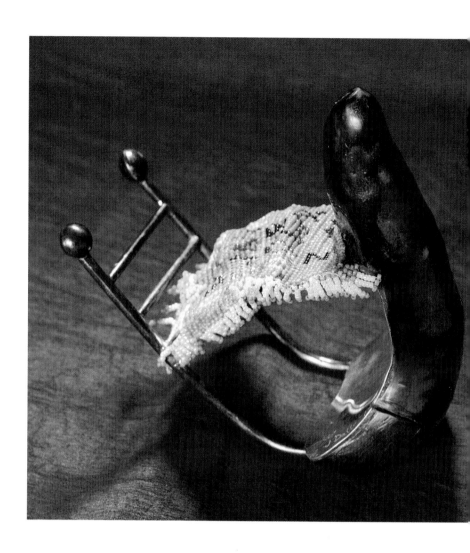

*That's How it Looks
to a Little Kid*
5 x 6 x 3 in.; forged
copper, fabricated
brass, silver, copper;
loom beaded with
14/0 seed beads

In the Garden of Beadin'
21 x 21 x 17 in.; 6/0, 10/0, and 11/0 seed beads, pressed glass leaves and flowers, Ultra Suede, clothesline, florist wire, and wire basket; various bead weaving and bead embroidery techniques (see p. 38)

JoAnn Feher

JoAnn credits beading with changing her life. She loves the way a mound of beads turns into a finished piece in her hands and receives great joy from the process. Her goal is that the joy she feels is transmitted by the humorous, whimsical nature of her work. She was inspired to begin beading by seeing Joyce Scott's work four years ago. She has since studied with David Chatt.

Nancy Eha

Although Nancy has been a bead artist for several years, *In the Garden of Beadin'* is her first piece to replicate objects as they appear in the real world. The piece is a humorous reflection on her relationship with beadwork. She says she was lured in by the lush color, texture, and sparkle and quickly succumbed to the disease of beadaholism. "As creating labor-intensive bead sculpture becomes the focus of my energies, I lose my balance and become consumed by my fascination with beads." That's why Nancy's leg and hair protrude from the mouth of her beaded Venus fly trap (detail above).

Nancy constructed the base of this piece by weaving Ultra Suede strips through a wire basket and sewing on 4,000 glass leaves and flowers. She constructed the large leaves and tropical flowers with right-angle weave and textile-beaded embellishment.

Garden Party
9 x 12 x 1 in.; seed beads, pressed and molded glass leaves and grapes; woven in flat and three-dimensional hollow peyote stitch

Jacqui B. Fehl

Jacqui considers herself a relatively new beader, having been working in the medium for only two years. She began beading to fill in the long hours of waiting on the set of the television sit-com where she works, but she has become so obsessed that she sometimes beads even in bed. *The Bride* was made on a papier-mâché base that she painted with acrylics and embellished with decoupage images. She hand set most of the beads and seed beads with tweezers into glue over two and a half months.

The Bride
18 x 25 x 5 in.; papier-mâché base, acrylics, decoupage images, beads of various sizes, glue

Diane Fitzgerald

Diane was drawn to beads ten years ago. Their transparency and reflectivity and the ability to connect them with thread satisfies her soul. She loves the feeling of them in her hands, playing with the color, and experiencing the rhythm of the work. Her desire is simply to create beautiful jewelry with beads—body adornment that delights both the wearer and the viewer. *Ginko Leaf Necklace* (p. 44) combines brick stitch for the leaves and peyote stitch for the cord.

Diane worked in collaboration with Valorie Harlow and Barbara McLean to create *The Three Furies*, their individual interpretations of the female forces from Greek mythology that avenge evil-doing.

The Three Furies
(each on life-size form)
18 x 30 x 10 in.; velvet bustiers, seed beads, abalone disks, fused glass pendants, feathers, silk flowers, metallic fabric, nylon thread, other beads, buttons, and sequins; using bead appliqué, fringing, and peyote stitch (left, pp. 42–43)

Ginko Leaf Necklace
1 x 36-in. necklace;
Japanese cylinder
beads, seed beads,
nylon beading thread,
and satin cord;
worked in tubular
peyote stitch and
brick stitch

Susan Etcoff Fraerman

Although Susan has only been beading for two years, she is deeply immersed in the art, having spent over 500 hours on *Family Tree*. She challenges herself each day to "see the forest and the trees"—to shift focus from the exquisite, minute detail of each bead to the message and shape of the piece as a whole. The inspiration for *Family Tree* came from a photograph of her great-grandmother, who died young, leaving a legacy of unanswered questions. Susan began to create the gown, the tree, in the autumn while driving through the Blue Ridge Mountains, so the richness of the turning leaves inspired her color choice. She modeled the hem of the gown, the base of the tree, after the winter grasses outside her window.

Family Tree
6 x 13 x 4 in.;
**found fiber-
board object,
seed beads,
gold Paris
dust, semi-pre-
cious stones,
coated wire,
and nylon
thread;
worked in
right angle
weave and
tubular peyote
stitch**

Jocelyn S. Giles

Jocelyn loves every facet of bead-work—from concept and design to tying the last knot. For her, beads are "magic," and she has been beading for over 20 years. She credits Virginia Blakelock's book, *Those Bad, Bad Beads*, with inspiring her to take her work further, saying, "Although beadwork is an ancient art, we are in a time of taking it into new dimensions—very exciting." *Pollen Chain*, a piece about her struggle with allergies, was a breakthrough for Jocelyn. She let it go where it needed to, not demanding that it turn out "pretty."

Pollen Chain
14 x 51 x 14 in.; 11/0 and 6/0 seed beads, string, wire, polymer clay, color Xerox images, paint, and flashlight; worked in variations on quadruple helix, peyote, and brick stitch

Swimming with the Big Fish
10 x 15 x 10 in.; seed beads, 5mm beads, and Plexiglas form onto which beads are
strung; figure and fish worked in peyote stitch (see p. 48)

Patty Haberman

Patty's work is influenced by the events in her life, both large and small. She also credits Joyce Scott with providing great inspiration and influence since she began beading in 1993. She enjoys the repetitive act of stitching beads, which relaxes her and gives her time to think about where the piece is going and what the next piece will be.

Swimming with the Big Fish came from her feelings of being overwhelmed by work, home, family, and the struggle to make art while juggling everything else. She decided just to quit worrying and take the plunge. Watching the vigilance of two verdins building a nest outside her dining room window inspired *Building a Home*. And *Right Knee, Left Knee, Two New Knees* is about her father's knee-replacement surgery.

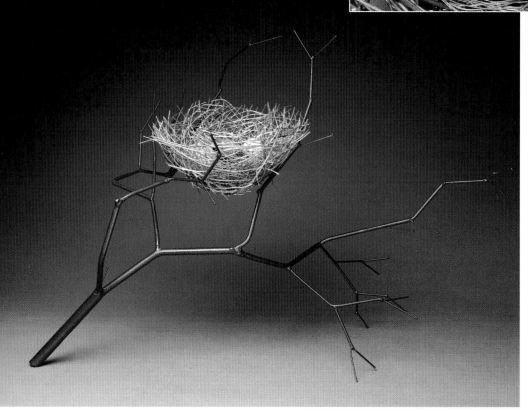

Building a Home
22 x 18 x 16 in.; seed beads, wooden eggs, welded steel frame, and steel, copper, and brass wire; eggs worked in peyote stitch, nest made by entwining wires

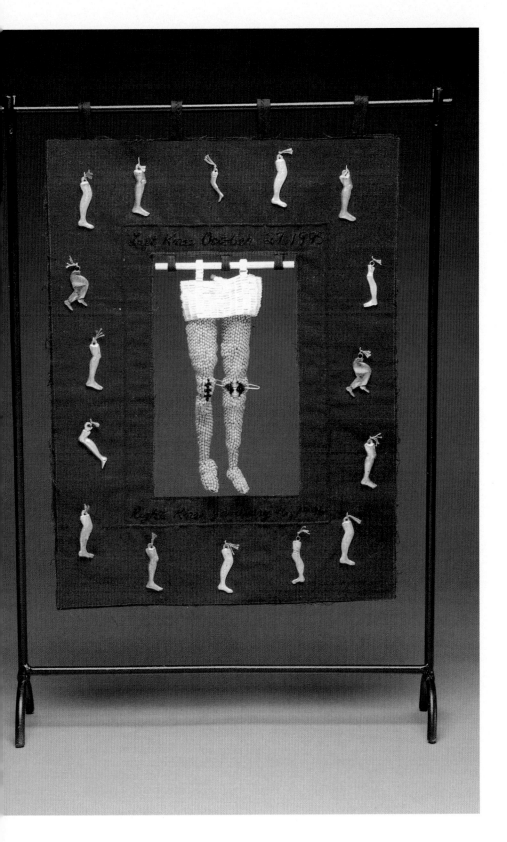

Right Knee, Left Knee, Two New Knees
12 x 17 x 3 in. seed beads, bugle beads, fabric, and *milagros* on welded steel frame; legs worked in peyote stitch, hospital gown in square stitch, and machine sewn and hand embroidered fabric

Valorie Harlow

Valorie finds great satisfaction in "taking a speck of glass and giving it life." She loves to create the parts of her bead sculptures then watch them come together, usually over a period of about six months. Her primary influence comes from her wonderful teachers and friends. When she made *Hot Line*, she was thinking about how people communicate and the balancing act between excitement and disappointment in intimate relationships.

Kathryn Harris

Kathryn thinks of her jewelry as personifications of women and strives to give each the right name. Because of its soft, feminine colors and the fact that it is made of beads collected in Paris, *Colette* is named for her favorite author.

Kathryn has been beading for five years and now uses wire exclusively with beads. She creates beadwork as an antidote to sadness; the color and light of the beads mean joy and freedom to her. In *Zazou* she joined ribbons of bugle beads with additional bugles to imitate faggot-stitch embroidery. Colors are different on each side of the triangular necklace but interlace at the corners.

Hot Line
10 x 8 x 8 in.;
seed beads
worked in peyote stitch (left)

Colette
necklace worn
doubled 6 x 9 x
1 in.; glass
beads, wire,
and metal drop
and vintage
clasp joined
with off-loom
weaving and
braiding

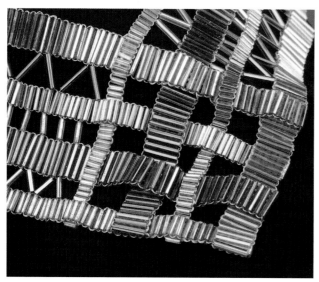

Mimi Holmes

Mimi's bead embroidered and densely embellished forms come from her dreams and "all the art I've ever seen, especially African." She began making them in 1982 from a need to manifest her ideas in tangible form. Her greatest joy comes from seeing a piece finished and getting people's reactions to it. A pragmatic artist, she says she likes the richness of beads and their inexpensiveness. *Weighted with Desire,* she says, "is about loving someone and how that desire rises up. The 'foot' is a 'penis' that rises into the air unless it is held down with the lead fishing weights wrapped around it."

Zazou
necklace 11 x 10 x 2½ in.; glass beads and wire joined with off-loom weaving

Weighted with Desire
11 x 6 x 4½ in.; figure: electrical
wire armature, batting, cotton fabric; embellishment: glass, caulk (to
glue glass) and handsewn beads,
shells, metal findings, and sequins

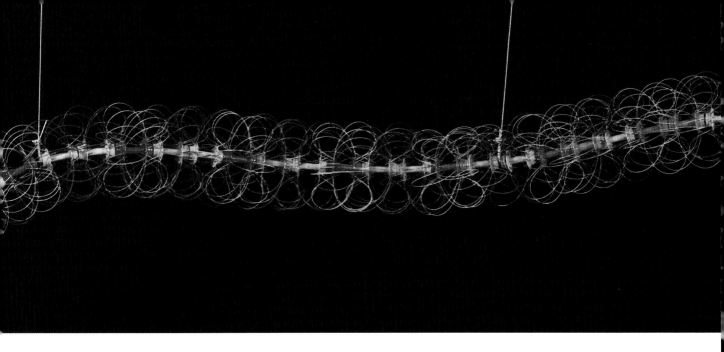

John W. Lefelhocz

John works in many media and gets most of his best ideas while riding his bicycle on country roads. He is interested in repetitive forms, saying "Subtle pattern changes make immense contributions to the overall effect of the work." His greatest thrill comes when a work is almost finished and he realizes that it is stronger than his mental images.

Discovering beadwork in the last year has re-sparked his interest in three-dimensional forms with intermingling peripheries. *One Month, One Week, and One Day* asks the viewer to think of all the other pierced objects that are possible "beads." John wonders whether the wheel might not have been an extension of the bead and says, "I'm just sending the wheel back to the bead."

One Month, One Week, and One Day
131 x 25 x 21 in.; bent ⅜-in. steel rod, bicycle hubs and spokes, gloss enamel paint, and other hardware parts; each hub painted, spokes threaded then painted before assembling on center rod

Richard LeMieux

Richard seeks quiet and contemplation, and his work has been most influenced by the discourses and meditations of Osho. He has been working with beads for more than 25 years and says his work has gone from being beaded things about his paintings to paintings in their own right. What he enjoys most about his bead art, he says, is "living in its presence." Because the cross has been a loaded image since prehistory, Richard feels that it is worth examination outside our cultural conditioning.

Cross
22 x 22 x 1 in.;
loom-woven seed
beads and acrylic
paint

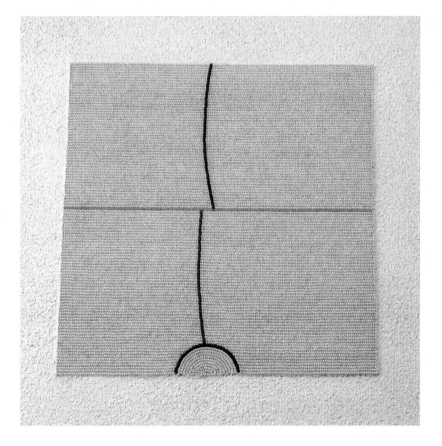

Cross
22 x 22 x 1 in.;
loom-woven seed
beads and acrylic
paint

Laura Leonard

Laura's art is about simple, everyday life—"Those moments of whimsy and playfulness that seemed to be everywhere when I was a girl. It's just the way I see the world." She has been beading for five years and says her greatest pleasure comes from finishing a piece, "After working on one for months, I am mystified by the results." Her strongest influence comes from her teachers, Diane Fitzgerald, Joyce Scott, and David Chatt.

Woman Who Runs with Poodles
15 x 19 x 15 in.; 14/0, 11/0, and 10/0 seed beads, wire, cotton knit, batting, rhinestones, and leather; sewn and worked in peyote stitch and bead embroidery

Lisa Lew

Lisa began beading at age 10 and feels beads have chosen her as much as she has chosen them. She creates painterly work with seed beads exclusively, having no desire to make jewelry or other types of ornamentation. Lisa works without a pattern and considers her bead embroidery an homage to beaders of the past. *The Pileated* was inspired by a pileated woodpecker who began frequenting her cabin just when she was trying to develop an idea for a new work. She assumed he wanted to be included (see p. 58).

The Pileated
19 x 19 x 1½ in.;
seed beads back-
stitched onto suede,
then secured on a
wooden hoop with
foam inserts

Eleanor Lux

Eleanor supports herself as a commissioned fiber artist, weaving wall pieces, rugs, and window shades. But she says that beading is her first love, and she has been doing it the way some people chain smoke for the last four years. Asked what her favorite part of beadwork is, she answers, "I love it all, but touching the work as it progresses is a special joy." She comments that the greatest challenge in beadwork is choosing the right seed beads because the ever-changing light is such an important part of each piece.

Trying to get away from everything she created having a strong sexual component, Eleanor thought, "What else is there but food?" The result was *Pasta Again* and *How to Separate an Egg*. She loves watching her Italian husband lift the limp spaghetti from the boiling water. When she finished this piece, she realized she loved it because the pasta looks like woven and knotted cloth. *How to Separate an Egg* was inspired by a new friend, who made an egg separator every day in wire-bending class.

How to Separate an Egg
3 x 12 x 3 in.; wire separator, antique crystals, and seed beads; worked in peyote stitch

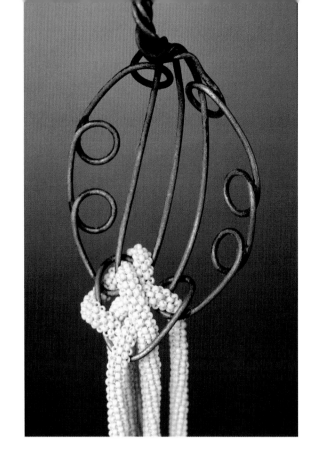

Pasta Again
3 x 15 x 3 in.; wire spoon and seed beads;
worked in peyote stitch

Liz Manfredini

Liz loves the feel of the seed beads as she works with them and the visual pleasure of color and emerging form. "I am drunk with beads!" she says. "What more is there to say?" Over the six years she has been beading her interest has shifted from creating jewelry to creating small sculptures. Liz is known for her perfectionism; she will rip out a piece as many times as it takes to achieve the form she wants. She works surrounded by dogs and folk art from around the world as she endeavors to communicate her joy in life, her sense of humor, and her questions. For her, humor is a saving grace—the only hope for sanity.

The Dairy Queen
10 x 9 x 4 in.;
glass seed
beads over
wire and clay;
worked pri-
marily in pey-
ote stitch.
Photo by Joe
Manfredini

NanC Meinhardt

NanC says that she doesn't plan her pieces. Rather, she meets them along the way as she travels her internal universe. She uses making art to express psychological phenomena that are both personal and universal. She has been beading for six years but making art full time for 15 years.

In *Let Me In/Let Me Out Family*, she used the mask format to express the different adaptations a mythical family might adopt as they struggle to become individuals.

Hiding in her Mother's Skirts began with a fragment of a slide of one of NanC's paintings that she heat-transferred to fabric. This piece, she says, meandered through recollections of being in and around her mother's skirt.

NanC thinks of a "vessel" as a container with the capacity to hold objects, memories, feelings, and fantasies, including the creative process itself. In *Fable Vessel*, she created a holding environment in which mythical characters interact with light, color, and the very walls of the structure, inviting the viewer to enter the story and create his/her own fable.

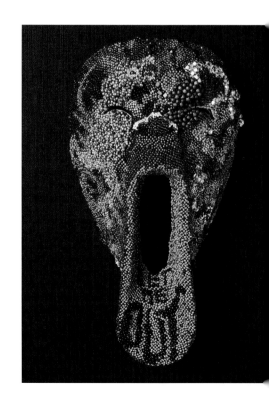

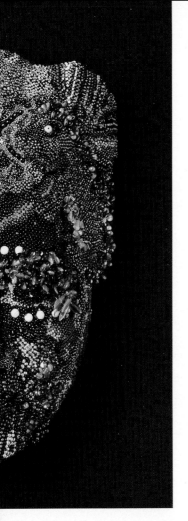

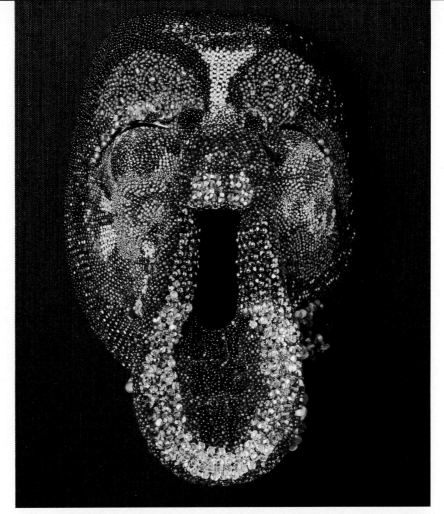

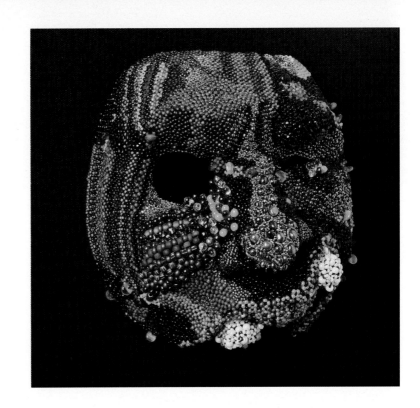

*Let Me In/
Let Me Out Family*
63 x 18 x 6 in.; seed
beads, other glass
beads, 22 kt gold 22/0
seed beads, wood, silk
and nylon threads;
joined with free-form
right-angle weave

Hiding in her Mother's Skirts
8 x 8 x 9 in.; glass beads,
nylon and cotton threads,
satin, interfacing, metal,
and suede; worked with
free-form right-angle
weave, peyote stitch,
applied beads, embroidery,
and photo heat transfer

Fable Vessel
14 x 8½ x 12 in.; glass
beads, nylon and silk
threads, and muslin;
worked with brick, pey-
ote, and square
stitches; applied beads;
right-angle weave; and
bead stringing (right)

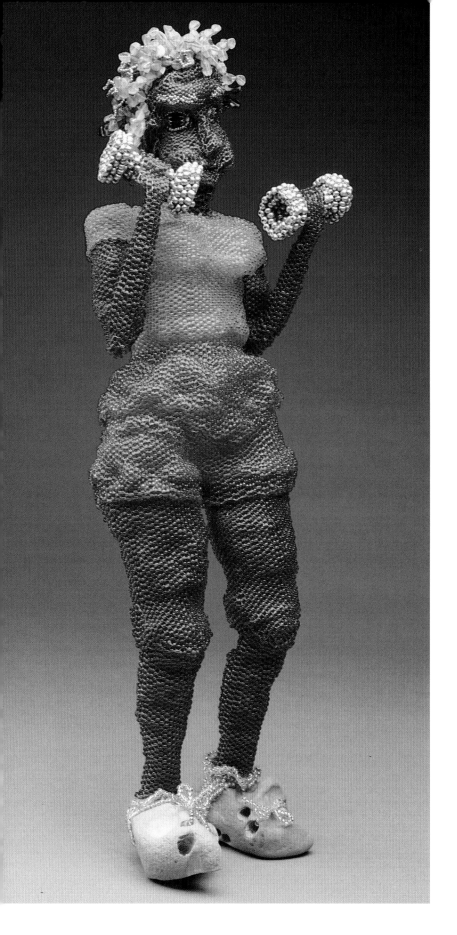

Ann Terepaugh Mitchell

A class with Joyce Scott and the color, texture, and light in beads got Ann hooked six years ago. Her favorite aspect of beadwork is the moment when a figure seems to come alive.

Refugees was inspired by a photo of a line of Rwandan women carrying large bundles of wood on their backs. Ann first thought about how their cumbersome burdens, intended for shelter and fire, provided a purpose for moving ahead with careful balance. Then she thought about how we are all refugees of the spirit.

Dumbbell came out of a spa week where Ann and a friend most enjoyed the dumbbell class because the teacher was so funny.

The Perm is about the freedom of the mind. According to Ann, "Although someone is changing the appearance and quality of the woman's hair, the real transformation is happening within her mind."

Dumbbell
5¼ x 13 x 4 in.; seed beads and rocks; worked in peyote stitch

Refugees
24 x 8 x 6 in.; seed beads,
old apothecary bottles,
and rocks; worked in pey-
ote stitch

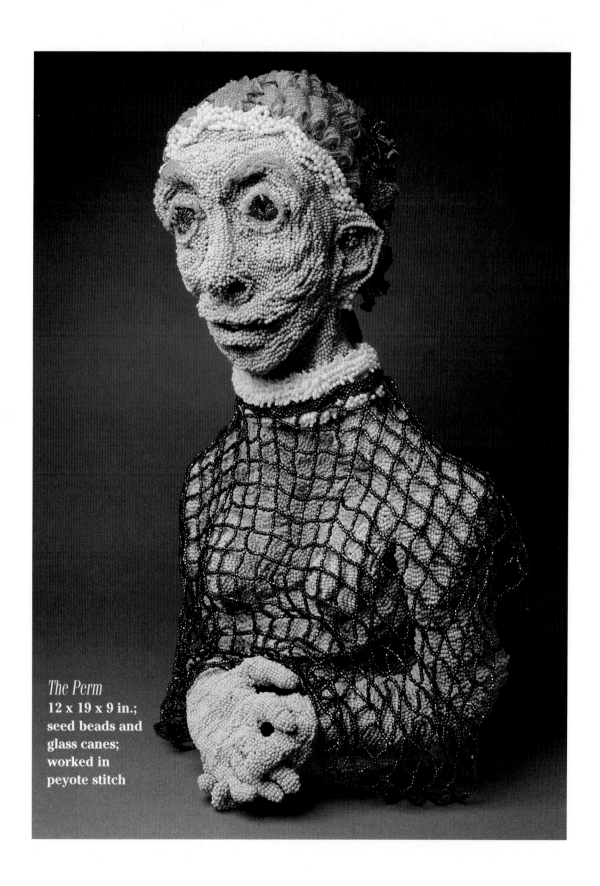

The Perm
**12 x 19 x 9 in.;
seed beads and
glass canes;
worked in
peyote stitch**

Soaked
16 x 24 x 10 in.;
dyed sponges;
peyote stitched
with fishing line

Nicole Nagel

Nicole is fascinated by the way so many individual components come together in beadwork to create a whole. In her bead art, she constantly pushes the boundaries of what we assume to be possible and impossible, challenging the idea of what people consider to be a bead. For her, the more unlikely it is that a material can be strung and woven together, the more interesting it becomes. She says, "It is the collision between known objects and the unknown product that inspires me to create. When I cross the boundaries of what is assumed, that is truly an enigma that menaces the mind."

Lisa Niforos

Lisa wants the details, which are usually drawn from nature, to be the focus of her pieces. She uses layers of beads as surface embellishment on her own blown sculptural glass forms. For her, the meditative act of beadweaving counterbalances the physically demanding process of blowing glass. Her greatest pleasure comes from making something out of nothing. Credit goes to Joyce Scott, who showed her how to bead her blown-glass beads and use them as a sculptural medium and who taught her to approach a situation as an opportunity.

Gorgon Medusa
6 x 4½ x 5 in.;
blown-glass form
embellished with
glued and wired
seed beads

Bargain Without Knowing
8 x 15 in.; seed beads joined in peyote stitch for tree and leaves, kinky fringe roots, charms, and larger beads

Jan Nix-Westhoff

Jan is a graphic artist who has been beading for the past three years. Of her beadwork she says, "My goals have changed from having to please others. My beadwork is just mine. It only has to make sense to me." The thing she likes most about beads is their tactile, dimensional quality, and her favorite part of a project is the beginning—because at this point the work can only be a success.

Bargain Without Knowing is filled with Jan's personal symbolism. The tree represents her, or all women. This is its summer, and it is still growing, not yet having blossomed or reached its full potential. She considers the roots especially interesting because they represent what people don't see but what nourishes her and keeps her growing even if the top is damaged. Charms reflect personal attributes and interests, and the lock suggests what she keeps hidden about herself. The snake represents the distractions that keep her from what is important in life.

Masquerade features many polymer clay masks that represent different cultural traits and emotions. Jan says, "These beady-eyed participants have chosen these masks for a reason known only to them."

Masquerade
13 x 12 in.; bugle bead collar in Comanche ladder; polymer clay masks embellished with horsehair, metallic glaze, pearl cotton, feathers, and copper wire; all joined with seed beads in free-form peyote stitch

Darkness
7 x 9 x 7 in.; seed
beads strung then
glued onto a gourd;
inside of gourd
painted with
acrylics

Colleen O'Rourke

Colleen initially chose to work with beads for their conve-
nience. She has a very small space in which to work and needs
to be able to clean up easily. However, she finds the process of
sewing or gluing almost meditative and has been beading 10 to
40 hours a week for six years. She is most influenced by African
and Native American art, her mother, Lynne O'Rourke, and
Joyce Scott. *Darkness* is the fourth beaded gourd in her ongoing series, and she says, "The image of a woman in an unde-
fined space is a recurring theme."

Row House #14
10 x 15½ x 1 in.; assorted found objects, velvet, metal; each object made into a bead and hand-stitched to velvet then metal, holes drilled for stitches as needed (above)

Row House #15
10 x 15½ x 1 in.; assorted found objects, velvet, metal; each object made into a bead and hand-stitched to velvet then metal, holes drilled for stitches as needed (right)

Amy Orr

Amy says that beads just seem right. She has worked with many media and finds beads the most expressive and most comfortable. In the four years that she has been beading she says that her pieces have become more intricate and obsessive. Her inspiration comes from the frantic pace of city living, and the stitching process, with all its monotony, gives her more pleasure and peace than she can express. "Stitching enchants me. I tell myself the stories about city life as I work. The finished pieces are lighthearted portrayals of despair, celebrations of survival," she says.

Amy lives in Philadelphia, a city of row houses, and intends her work to reflect social and visual patterns of community. *Row House #14* and *#15* are from a series in progress. In them elegant glass beads contrast with unexpected lead pellets and shot-up aluminum for a classical city image of the late 1990s. Amy says, "We are bombarded with elements of hope, pleasure, escape, and despair. My studio is full of visual delights: stuff people turn away from, throw away, step over, and try not to touch. These artifacts and their sociological implications are materials for making art from refuse and sense from senselessness."

Kristen Frantzen Orr

Seen in a Telescope
22-in.-long necklace; lampworked glass beads: two with gold foil and acid-etched, two with frits and foil encased in clear; hand-made, gold-plated copper wire bead and tubular chain

Kristen has been making lampworked glass beads since 1993 and feels her art career has come full circle back to watercolor, where she started. Now she uses watercolor-like layering techniques in molten glass to create depth and capture the play of light in colors of great clarity. She is particularly drawn to beads, saying, "Beads are intimate and personal. In addition to being visually pleasing, they feel good to wear and to hold." The challenge of making jewelry with her own glass beads is keeping the design light enough to be wearable.

Seen in a Telescope is Kristen's memory of a glimpse of the heavens with their sparkling celestial mysteries. *Seen in the Dishpan* brings such beauty just a little closer. Kristen asks, "Have you ever looked at some commonplace thing and suddenly seen it in a different way? This piece is my attempt to capture such a moment and to encourage others to pause and notice the beauty in ordinary things."

Seen in the Dishpan
16-in.-long necklace; lampworked glass beads and crocheted magnet-wire beads

Betty Pan

In the last five years Betty has gone from creating large-scale woven tapestries to miniature beadwork. Trained as a graphic artist, she finds beadwork intriguing because she starts with a single bead in mind and the design forms as she adds more. She is finally at peace when the finished design comes together. She typically spends about a week on a piece like *Kaleidoscope*.

Kaleidoscope
17½ x 13 in. in a free-standing frame; Japanese cylinder beads worked in brick stitch

If I Were Going

9 x 11 x 3 in.; hand-sewn doll form of cotton fabric, zipper heads and seed beads attached with various simple stitches (left)

Christy Puetz

Christy has been making soft sculpture, bead-covered doll forms for about seven years. Instead of writing a story, she says she places the story on a nontraditional doll form covered with beads and other materials. The dolls express her many emotions: *Murtha Bacon Salmo* tells of hard work, pride, support, and drive; and *Auburn Beauty* reflects contemplation, appreciation, problems, and pride. But the overall feeling Christy wishes to convey through the dolls is pleasure.

Murtha Bacon Salmo

10 x 11 x 4 in.; hand-sewn doll form of cotton fabric and seed beads attached with various simple stitches (right)

Auburn Beauty
4½ x 12 x 4 in.; hand-sewn doll form of cotton fabric and seed beads attached with various simple stitches and fringe

Madelyn C. Ricks

A full-time clay artist for over 15 years, Madelyn had thought about changing media for some time because of health problems. When she saw *The New Beadwork* a few years ago, she knew she'd found what she wanted. She says, "Every day with beads is such fun, I can't wait to get started in the morning." She hopes her work can bring equal pleasure to the viewer.

**Millennium
Celebration
Goblet**
9 x 12 x 6 in.;
glass ball and
Japanese
cylinder
beads worked
in peyote
stitch

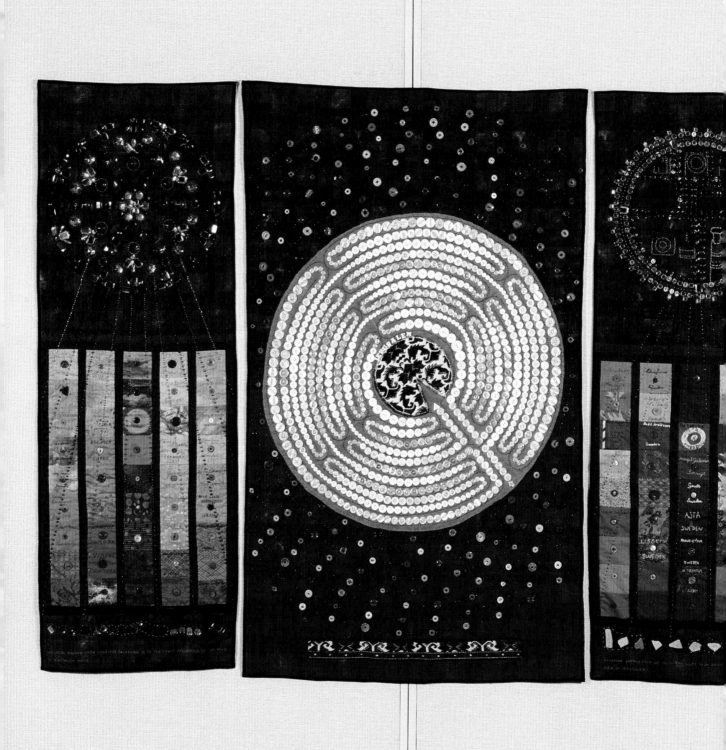

The Road to Jerusalem

74 x 54 in.; sweat-shirt knit, hand embroidered cotton fabrics, Bukhara cap embroidery, tulle, buttons, rhinestones, glass beads, and 12th century ceramic shards; hand quilted through beads and buttons (left)

Dust into Gold

15 x 15 in.; disposable vacuum cleaner bag, buttons, beads, and charms; hand quilted through golden beads

Rachel Roggel

The properties of buttons—their color, shape, size, texture, and material—are Rachel's artistic language. For four years, she has been challenging the concept of "quilt" by constructing hers of sweatshirt and tee-shirt material and hand sewing the designs to their surfaces in buttons. She describes her studio as a 70,000-button mess and says she doesn't lose her buttons, but her clothes are usually missing one.

She is also an internet addict, which gave her the impetus for her *Pilgrimage to Jerusalem* series. Rachel's home is a mile from Mt. Gaudii, where crusaders got their first sight of Jerusalem almost 900 years ago. That fact, and the 3,000th anniversary of the city inspired her to create a series of signature quilts commemorating the act of pilgrimage. *The Road to Jerusalem* re-creates a 13th century labyrinth on the floor of Chartres cathedral. Medieval pilgrims would walk the labyrinth to substitute for the actual journey. Rachel's labyrinth is made from buttons sent to her by virtual pilgrims from the internet. By finger-tracing it, the viewer also becomes a pilgrim to Jerusalem.

Dust into Gold is a more personal statement. Her father was a goldsmith, and every year her parents would send the dust swept from the floor to a refinery to recover a pound of gold. Rachel's own vacuum cleaner bags also contain a gold mine—the buttons and beads from her studio carpet.

Ruth Marie Satterlee

"Beads chose me," says Ruth Marie. Since she works improvisationally, without a specific goal, she finds constant excitement in the process of stitching each bead and seeing what happens. That's how her *Beaded Beads* were created. With each one, she asks herself, "If I make this 'mistake' and keep repeating it, what will happen? If I mix these colors that I'm not comfortable using, what will happen?" Ruth Marie loves her beaded beads but sees her greatest challenge in beading as moving beyond beautiful embellishment. She hopes to be able to make pieces with many levels of meaning that initially attract viewers with color and shape, then pull them in deeper. She wants to create work that reveals deep feelings, that is political, and that offers sometimes unconventional answers.

Beaded Beads
sizes range from ¾ to 2¼ in.; seed beads, glass beads, and pearls; woven with peyote stitch and right-angle weave

Midwest Mecca
23 x 23 x 2 in.;
fabric, beads,
found objects,
paint, Fome Core,
wood

Pamela Schloff

Pamela has been a textile artist for 20 years and added beading to her work two years ago. She likes the way adding these small bits of color invites the viewer to come closer. She says that the glint of beads, especially in low light, creates an illusion of movement. *Midwest Mecca*, the first in her series of shrines to everyday existence, was created by machine piecing fabric, hand sewing beads to the fabric then mounting the whole over a framework of Fome Core and wood.

Desert Dust Devils
1 x 24 x 1 in.;
polymer clay
beads strung on
rawhide

Carol Shelton

A polymer clay artist since 1989, Carol is drawn first to color and second to movement in her beadwork. She makes her own beads and says that a piece takes "embarrassingly long" to make because of the many hours involved in mixing colors and playing with their interactions. For the beads in *Desert Dust Devils* she first built graduated color blocks. Then she created multiple-strip slabs from each color block. Next she placed two different slabs together, reduced, cut, stacked, and reduced many times until the colors changed. Finally, she cut narrow strips from the slab and wound them around each bead base to create a spiral pattern. Carol says she's especially fond of the spiral form because it is dynamic, "always moving, always changing."

Nancy Smeltzer

Nancy has been making art quilts for 16 years and has added beads and buttons to them with increasing elaboration for the past eight years. In *Jungle Garden* Nancy wanted to show the intense, searing sunlight in a lush jungle garden, but the busyness of the fabric kept overwhelming her. So she took it apart and rearranged it at least five times over a span of four years. Finally she had the bright idea of covering most of the surface with beads, and the piece began to gel for her. She says, "While beading this much surface area took forever, the slow process gave me a chance to calm my spirit so that the image on the quilt could blend. I just keep adding beads until the piece looks right." Nancy is particularly attracted to lined seed beads and says, "It's fun to imagine what it would be like to be inside the bead and see light coming through the different colored walls."

Jungle Garden
40 x 37 x 1 in.; fabric, glass and
plastic beads and buttons,
jewelry, metal studs; assembled
with machine appliqué and
embroidery, hand quilting and
embroidery, hand beading and
couching

Blue Gallé, Green Moss
7½ x 9¼ in. necklace; Art
Nouveau glass by Gallé,
Japanese seed beads, bugle
beads, antique button and
vintage glass nail heads;
worked with peyote and
brick stitches

Inspired by Iolite
19-in.-long necklace;
three-layer lamp-
worked glass beads
and 14kt gold beads
and clasp

Sandy Swirnoff

For Sandy, the pleasure and the challenge of beadwork are the same: making
the concept in her imagination come to
life. She loves the options of colors,
shapes, and sizes of beads and the inti-
macy of holding her work in her hands.
Sandy has been beading for five years
and comments that she started as a bead
stringer, but she is now using smaller and
smaller beads and more detail. A piece
usually takes her nine months of noncon-
tinuous work.

The challenge of *Blue Gallé, Green
Moss* was to set off a beautiful piece of
French Gallé art glass in a simple structure that would not detract from it. She
wanted to repeat the diagonal lines in the
glass but also to soften the geometric
lines and the hard glass by adding the
fluid seed bead moss.

Thalia Tringo

Thalia says she stumbled into making
beaded jewelry in 1990, and it changed
her life. She has since learned to make
glass beads, which she features in her
jewelry. Her two favorite processes are
sculpting hot glass in her lampworking
torch and playing with jewelry designs.

Inspired by Iolite is part of her *Tribute
to Stone* series in which she imitates or
evokes the colors of favorite semi-pre-
cious gemstones in lampworked beads. In
its highest grades, iolite is an intense
translucent blue-purple; and when held
to the light, it's hard to determine
whether it's more blue or purple. Thalia
says her glass beads don't look like iolite,
but they evoke the same sense of dueling
blues and purples.

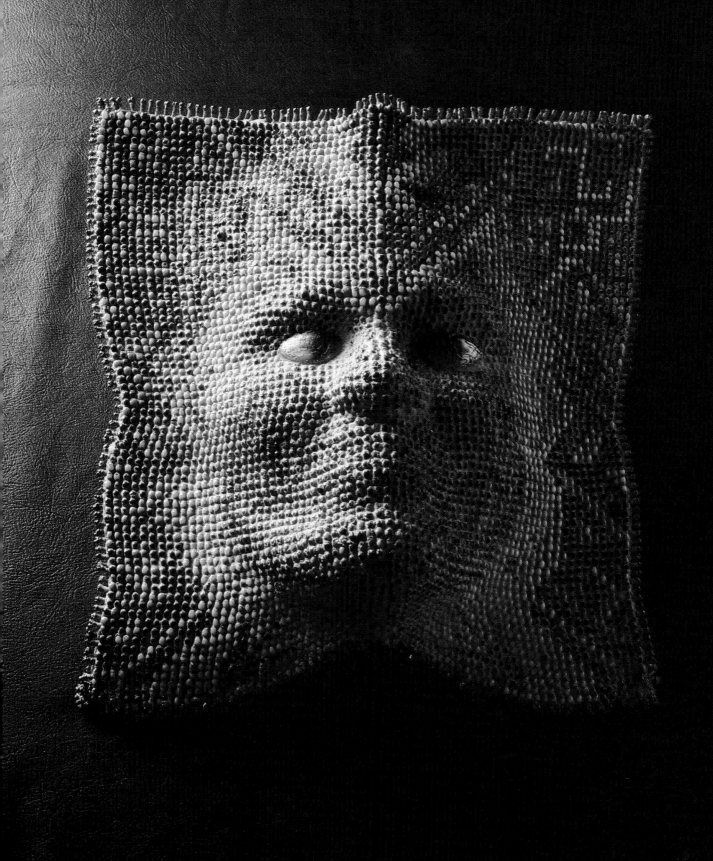

Carolyn Veerjee

Carolyn has always been fascinated by costumes, masks, beads, and sequins and has worked with beads since she was about 11. Her current work combines low-tech beadwork—she stitches glass beads to a sculpted brass wire mesh—with high-tech electroforming in a copper-plating solution. The piece is then patinated. Each piece takes three to four months to complete. She credits James Nagy for his technological guidance.

The brass wire mesh shape of *Ardent* is an imprint of Carolyn's own face.

Ardent
12 x 12 x 4 in.; glass beads, sculpted brass wire mesh, nylon thread, copper-plating solution, copper eyes

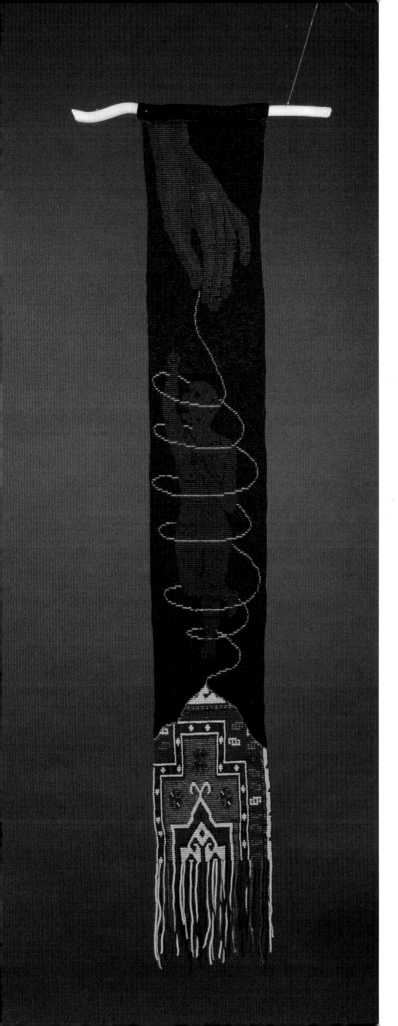

Sally Wassink

A writer and bead artist, Sally has been making large, loom-woven bead hangings since 1991. Because she works full time as well, her pieces take about six months to complete. She has been most influenced by *The New Beadwork*, bead artist Edward Derwent, and needlepoint artist D. R. Wagner.

Sally tries to build additional layers of meaning into each piece. For example, the background of *She Again* has her prose poem of the same name worked into it. When light shines through the piece, the words are obliterated and become simply a pattern of glowing light. *Spin*, she says, "Considers the creative spark, its relation to the divine, and the belief that it exists in everyone. It asks whether that spark can work through you to bring order out of chaos; will you spin out of control, or will you spin some meaningful order?"

Spin
5 x 36 in.; 11/0
seed beads
loom woven
and mounted on
a bleached stick

She Again
13 x 21 in.; 11/0
seed beads
loom woven
and mounted on
a wooden dowel

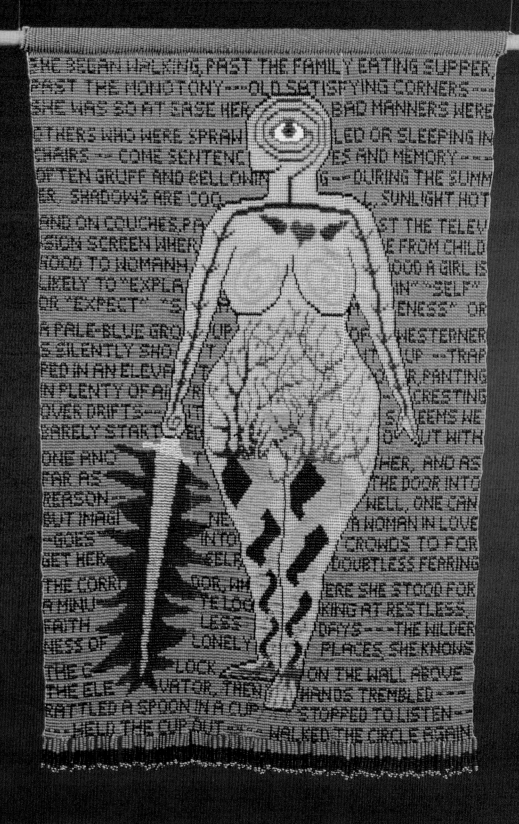

SHE BEGAN WALKING, PAST THE FAMILY EATING SUPPER, PAST THE MONOTONY---OLD SATISFYING CORNERS--- SHE WAS SO AT EASE HER   BAD MANNERS WERE OTHERS WHO WERE SPRAW   LED OR SLEEPING IN CHAIRS --- COME SENTENC   ES AND MEMORY--- OFTEN GRUFF AND BELLOWI   G---DURING THE SUMM ER, SHADOWS ARE COO   L, SUNLIGHT HOT AND ON COUCHES, PA   ST THE TELEV ISION SCREEN WHER   E FROM CHILD HOOD TO WOMANH   OOD A GIRL IS LIKELY TO "EXPLA   IN" "SELF" OR "EXPECT" "S   ENESS" OR A PALE-BLUE GRO   UP   OR WESTERNER S SILENTLY SHO   UP ---TRAP PED IN AN ELEVA   R, PANTING IN PLENTY OF A   CRESTING OVER DRIFTS---   S EEMS WE O UT WITH BARELY START   HER, AND AS ONE AND   THE DOOR INTO FAR AS   WELL, ONE CAN REASON---   A WOMAN IN LOVE BUT IMAGI   HE CROWDS TO FOR ---GOES INTO   DOUBTLESS FEARING GET HER SELF   THE CORR DOOR, AH   ERE SHE STOOD FOR A MINU TE LOO   KING AT RESTLESS FAITH LESS   DAYS ---THE WILDER NESS OF LONELY   PLACES, SHE KNOWS THE C LOCK   ON THE WALL ABOVE THE ELE VATOR, THEN   HANDS TREMBLED --- BATTLED A SPOON IN A CUP   STOPPED TO LISTEN--- ---HELD THE CUP OUT--- WALKED THE CIRCLE AGAIN

Dustin J. Wedekind

Dustin has been beading for three years. He loves buying beads and picking them for a piece. In his beadwork, he seeks to explore dualities. He explains that each bead is like an individual cell that combines with others to make a whole organism. The hardness of the glass is transformed into a flexible cloth, and opposing colors can be placed next to each other to intensify their luminosity. According to Dustin, "Sex is one of the greatest dualities in our lives and sexual identity is the main focus of my work. I use the seductive nature of beads to draw the viewer into these sexual representations."

Blue Glass
10 x 9 x 1 in.; 14/0 seed beads worked in square stitch and mounted on colored glass (above)

Twelve Bulge
8 x 10 x 1 in.; 11/0 seed beads worked in increasing and decreasing square stitch

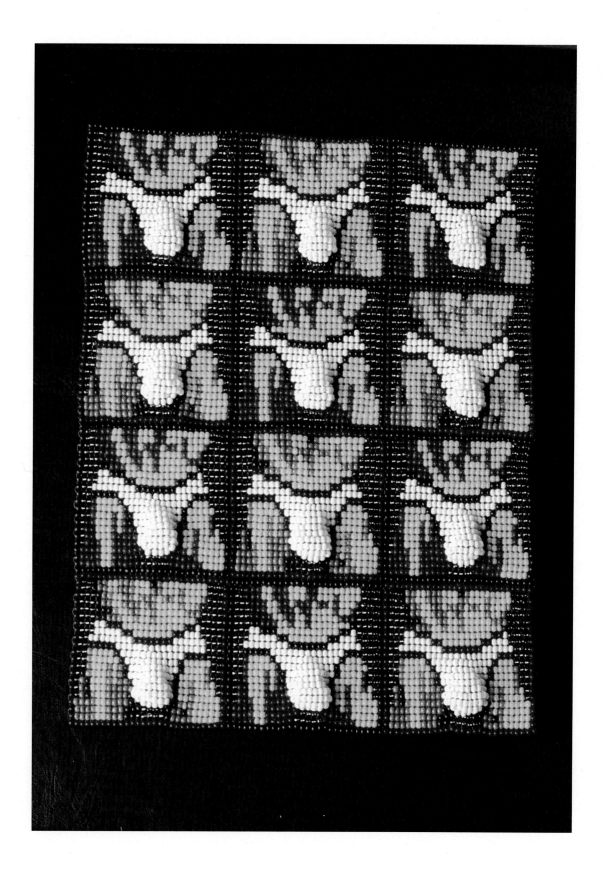

Alison F. Whittemore

Formerly a civil engineer, Alison gave it all up to make art. Her favorite part of working with beads is choosing them, and she loves how they make her feel like a kid playing. So, of course, the hardest part is knowing when to quit. She began with seed beads but has added polymer clay and surface design to her repertoire. For *Bean Pot* she went through her entire bead collection, pulling out all the beads she loved but couldn't figure out how to use. Then she glued them all to an old bean pot and placed it in the center of her table. Now she can enjoy her collection every day.

Bean Pot
10 x 10 x 10 in.;
ceramic bean
pot, beads,
buttons, gee-
gaws, glue

Michelle Williams

A weaver and fiber artist in the '70s, Michelle eventually found beads and was hooked. She stitches most of her beads onto cloth using couched bead embroidery, peyote stitch, right-angle weave, and square stitch, and stuffs the sculpture when beading is complete; all her pieces include a crystal at the core. She especially loves the fact that her work takes so long (two to nine months), that the process reflects her inner life, and that the piece evolves with a mind of its own. She feels that beading has helped her grow as a person and that by letting her inner feelings out she has come to understand life better.

Getting Ready took a short time to complete, but after showing it, Michelle wasn't satisfied and spent an additional nine months adding more and more beads.

On a family vacation in Costa Rica she was impressed by sloths in the wild and began *Sloth Girl's* face. Since it looked like a sloth, she added spiked fringe on the back to suggest the fungus and plant life that grows on sloths.

Sabotaging the Working Woman was Michelle's way of turning a distressing situation in a positive direction. She wanted the piece to have an inside so the viewer could find more, so she beaded a peyote-stitch basket and inset it. Then she beaded a baby and attached it with a beaded umbilical cord.

Getting Ready
6 x 6 x 5 in.; cotton cloth, thread, seed and antique beads, charms, a crystal, and a suede button; worked with peyote, right-angle weave, and square stitch

Sloth Girl
7 x 9 x 7 in.; cloth, thread, seed beads, and a crystal; worked with peyote stitch, couching, and spiked fringe (right)

Sabotaging the Working Woman
7 x 7 x 6½ in.; cotton, thread, suede, a crystal, dacron, glass beads, charms, and antique beads; worked with peyote stitch and couched bead embroidery

Laura Willits

Laura's goal is to change the way people see things. She works and travels at night and says, "Even the most mundane landscape can become movingly beautiful in the dark." *Span I* depicts a highway overpass on the north side of Minneapolis, MN. She weaves Czech and Japanese 11/0 seed beads on her homemade oak and brass loom, first drawing the image on her computer, which provides her with a gridded color printout. A beadweaver for about four years, Laura feels that the intense colors of glass seed beads reflect her interior vision more closely than paint or print. *Eclipse* is her response to a lunar eclipse visible in Seattle, WA, in spring 1997.

Eclipse
13 x 11 x 2 in.;
11/0 seed beads
and thread; loom
woven

Span I
13 x 11 x 2 in.; 11/0
seed beads and
thread; loom
woven

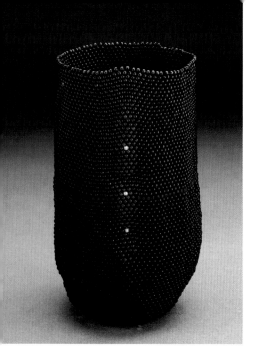

THE JURY

Jeannine Anderson

As one of three jurors, I enjoyed the privilege of working with Barbara Lee Smith and Joyce Scott, sharing viewpoints, comparing reactions and theories, and ultimately learning from each other, the jurying process, and the works we viewed. Our experience was further enhanced by the warm and generous hospitality of the Dairy Barn Southeastern Ohio Cultural Arts Center staff.

The works included in this exhibit represent only a portion of the entries. The process of selection began with an overall view. We narrowed down the large pool through several viewings, attempting to select pieces that would work together as a coherent exhibit. Our goals were to show the full range of diversity and flexibility within the bead medium and to show the strongest possible work. Our selection criteria included the following: Works had to be technically well crafted, conceptually mature and developed, sensitive to the language of the media, and visually interesting. I also looked for pieces that showed something of their maker—that were soulful.

The entries met some of our expectations, but also held many surprises. Sculptural beaded forms were well represented, whereas vessels were few. Many established bead artists were noticeably absent, and many exciting emerging artists appeared. One of our easiest and most unanimous decisions was the selection of award recipients. The three award-winning pieces—best of show *Refugees* by Ann Terepaugh Mitchell, best of Ohio *Cross* by Richard LeMieux, and most innovative use of the medium *Ardent* by Carolyn Veerjee—stood out from the group as well developed, individualistic, and emotionally evocative.

I believe the resulting exhibit displays a high level of creativity, intelligence, skill, and sensitivity on the part of these artists. May all who view the exhibit enjoy it, be challenged by it, and learn something of the contemporary bead medium.—*J.A.*

Blue Vertical
by Jeannine Anderson, 2 x 5 x 2 in.; glass seed beads and nylon thread assembled in a netting technique.
Photo by Mary Rezny

Sun Boat
by Barbara Lee Smith, 30 x 6–7 x 4 in.; printed, stitched melted, and fused synthetic materials. This boat might not last long in water, but it is intended to take the willing observer to another place. For Barbara, boats signify movement, mystery, and the art of letting go gracefully.
Photo by Tom Van Eynde

108

Barbara Lee Smith

That which delights me in art is not constrained by medium or technical facility. I respond to work that engages me on many levels: emotional, intellectual, visceral. I return to certain works in my memory and appreciate their power and ability to jar me into new insights. I acknowledge work that provokes. I may disagree with the visual "opinion" of the work, but I honor its ability to express that opinion. I admire work that appears to have been created in a timeless moment, that exceeds the boundaries of technique and materials and exists in a space of its own making.

When even some of the above happens to me as I help to select an exhibition, I feel honored to be part of the art-making process, that is, showing the finished work. On occasion, that magical moment occurred during the jurying of *Beadworks 1998*. I hope that this will be the first of a series of exhibitions that, over time, will help those who choose beads as their expressive medium to grow with this art form. I look forward to being engaged, provoked, amused, delighted, mystified, and moved by their works.—*B.L.S.*

P-Melon #1
by Joyce Scott, 13 x 20 x 10 in.; blown glass, glass beads, and thread. Photo by Kanui Takeno

Joyce Scott

As a beadworker for over 40 years, I'm heartened by the ongoing advances of this medium. Beadwork is everywhere!—all kinds and qualities of craftsmanship and invention. There is also a lot of crap. However, I believe it's all good because it expands the scope and capacity for artists to experiment and for the audience to experience.

The Dairy Barn and *Beadworks 1998* offers a wonderful opportunity to forward the critical discourse necessary to extend the field beyond its extraordinary genesis of ceremonial, tribal, and decorative arts. The contemporary approach to sculptural and wearable arts integrates the former while addressing universal issues and employing modern technologies and materials. This first step for the Dairy Barn surveys fine examples by both veterans and newcomers, exposing beadwork as a syncopated journey with generous rewards. Ain't life grand!—*J.S.*

THE DAIRY BARN

Welcome to the home of *Beadworks® 1998*! For more than 20 years the Dairy Barn Southeastern Ohio Cultural Arts Center, a nonprofit organization, has served as an exhibit venue for artists whose creative energies find voice in a wide variety of media. Our shows have attracted artists and visitors from all over the world.

When visitors approach the building, they see a wonderful example of early 20th century barn architecture resting atop a gently sloping hill with a stand of beautiful, mature trees in the background. The rustic appearance of the exterior is, however, in sharp contrast to the fully equipped 6,500 square-foot multipurpose gallery and the arts education center found inside.

The mission of the Dairy Barn Cultural Arts Center is to promote the arts, crafts, and cultural heritage of southeastern Ohio and to bring to the region the very best art from all over the world. While our exhibition history certainly includes paintings and sculptures, there has also been a strong emphasis on showcasing the creativity and strengths of artists who choose to work with materials and methods frequently associated with folk art and/or functional objects. The most notable of these is *Quilt National*, a series of biennial international exhibitions of art quilts—works that maintain the quilt's structural elements while expressing the artists' visions in the same way as more traditional art forms.

We have learned an important thing with 10 *Quilt Nationals* and with similar exhibitions of basketry, glass, and woodworking: There is a need for and an interest in exhibitions that present the artistry expressed through media that have often been considered the "poor cousins" of painting and sculpture. Not only has there been an increase in the number of visitors over the years, there has also been an equally obvious and significant change in the subtlety and sophistication of the work. It should be no surprise, therefore, that we are now turning our attention to the artistry of beadworkers and to the breadth of expression that they are producing.

Beadworks® 1998 features cutting-edge artwork in which beads are a primary element and transcend their customary role as simple adornment or embellishment. The exhibition consists of 81 pieces representing 54 artists. It includes many different approaches to beadwork, from jewelry to large-scale sculpture. There are works of whimsy as well as social commentary. As you read through this book, we hope you will be charmed and challenged by the exciting and unique artwork selected by jurors Jeannine Anderson, Joyce Scott, and Barbara Lee Smith. All leaders in their fields, their experience and insight has produced a novel exhibit of this rapidly evolving art form.

There is no question that producing a show of this quality and size requires a great deal of support, financial and otherwise. We would like to acknowledge the generous contributions of our sponsors: the *Athens Ohio Messenger*; Beads & Things (Athens, Ohio); Beadworks International, Inc. (Norwalk, Connecticut); Byzantium (Columbus, Ohio); the City of Athens; Larry Conrath Realty (Athens, Ohio); Miyuki Shoji Co., Ltd., manufacturers and suppliers of glass beads, Delica beads, Beads & Crafts (Tokyo, Japan); and the Ohio Arts Council. We would also like to thank Alice Korach, who guided the production of this book to completion, and the staff of Kalmbach Publishing Co. for transforming our vision into a beautiful, hard-bound reality. We are also grateful to the jurors and, of course, to all the artists who shared their work with us. Without those talented people, *Beadworks® 1998* would not exist. The Dairy Barn Southeastern Ohio Cultural Arts Center is fortunate to have the support of its hundreds of members, the Athens community, and dozens of volunteers. Without this assistance, we could not succeed in our mission of providing original exhibits, educational programs, festivals, and touring exhibits.

Those unable to visit the Dairy Barn in person can sample the variety of our past and current exhibitions through our site on the World Wide Web (http://www.eurekanet.com/~dbarn). For a calendar of events or information about the Dairy Barn's current and future programs, visit the web site or contact us at the Dairy Barn Cultural Arts Center, PO Box 747, Athens, OH 45701-0747 USA; phone (740) 592-4981; fax (740) 592-5090; e-mail dbarn@eurekanet.com.

Susan Cole Urano,
Executive Director

BIBLIOGRAPHY

Books

Allen, Jamey D. *Five Artists—Five Directions in Polymer Clay*. Rockville, MD: Flower Valley Press, 1995.

Ashcroft, Pierrette Brown and Lindly Haunani. *Artists At Work: Polymer Clay Comes of Age*. Rockville, MD: Flower Valley Press, 1996.

Barth, Georg J. *Native American Beadwork*. Stevens Point, WI: R. Schneider, Publishers, 1993.

Blakelock, Virginia. *Those Bad, Bad Beads*. Virginia Blakelock, POB 2840, Wilsonville, OR 97070, 1990.

Borel, France. *The Splendor of Ethnic Jewelry*. New York: Harry N. Abrams, Inc., 1994.

Campbell-Harding, Valerie and Pamela Watts. *Bead Embroidery*. Berkeley, CA: Lacis Publications, 1993.

Casey, Tina. *Creating Extraordinary Beads from Ordinary Materials*. Cincinnati, OH: North Light Books, F&W Publications, Inc., 1997.

Cera, Deanna Farneti, ed. *Jewels of Fantasy: Costume Jewelry of the 20th Century*. 1991. English version: New York: Harry N. Abrams, Inc., 1992.

Cook, Jeannette and Vicki Star. *Beady Eyed Women's Guide to Exquisite Beadwork* (5 volumes, including): *A Bead & Weave Primer* and *A Fringe & Edge, Tassel & Trim Primer*. Jeannette Cook, POB 60691, San Diego, CA, 1994–.

Dierks, Leslie. *Creative Clay Jewelry*. Asheville, NC: Lark Books, 1994.

Dubin, Lois Sherr. *The History of Beads*. New York: Harry N. Abrams, Inc., 1987.

Dunham, Bandu Scott. *Contemporary Lampworking*. First Edition, 1994; Second Edition. Salusa Glassworks, POB 2354, Prescott, AZ 86302, 1997.

Elbe, Barbara. *Beaded Images: Intricate Beaded Jewelry Using Brick Stitch* (1995) and *Back to Beadin'*. B.E.E. Publishing, 556 Hanland Ct., Redding, CA 96003, 1996.

Fisch, Arline M. *Textile Techniques in Metal*. Asheville, NC: Lark Books, 1996.

Fitzgerald, Diane. *Contemporary Beadwork I: Counted and Charted Patterns for Flat Peyote Stitch* (and other titles). Beautiful Beads, 115 Hennepin Ave., Minneapolis, MN 55401, 1995.

Fitzgerald, Diane and Helen Banes. *Beads and Threads: A New Technique for Fiber Jewelry*. Rockville, MD: Flower Valley Press, 1993.

Ford, Steven and Leslie Dierks. *Creating with Polymer Clay*. Asheville, NC: Lark Books, 1996.

Forrington, Sandy. *Picot Lace: Innovative Beadwork*. Picot Press, POB 2298, Ft. Bragg, CA 95437, 1993.

Jenkins, Cindy. *Making Glass Beads*. Asheville, NC: Lark Books, 1997.

Jones, Julia. *The Beading Book*. Berkeley, CA: Lacis Publications, 1993.

Liu, Robert K. *Collectible Beads: A Universal Aesthetic*. Vista, CA: Ornament, Inc., 1995.

Monture, Joel. *The Complete Guide to Traditional Native American Beadwork*. New York: Collier Books, Macmillan Publishing Co., 1993.

Morris, Jean and Eleanor Preston-Whyte. *Speaking with Beads: Zulu Arts from Southern Africa*. New York: Thames and Hudson, 1994.

Moss, Kathlyn and Alice Scherer. *The New Beadwork*. New York: Harry N. Abrams, Inc., 1992.

Roche, Nan. *The New Clay* (and forthcoming *The New Clay II*). Rockville, MD: Flower Valley Press, 1991.

Root, Gineke. *Innovative Beaded Jewelry Techniques*. 1988. English version: Berkeley, CA: Lacis Publications, 1994.

Scott, Joyce. *Fearless Beadwork*. Visual Studies Workshop, 31 Prince St., Rochester, NY 14607, 1994.

Serena, Raffaella. *Berlin Work: Samplers & Embroidery of the Nineteenth Century*. 1991. English version: Berkeley, CA: Lacis Publications, 1996.

Starr, Sadie. *Beading with Seed Beads, Gem Stones & Cabochons*. Camp Verde, AZ: Shooting Starr Publications, 1993.

Stessin, Nicolette. *Beaded Amulet Purses*. Beadworld Publishing, POB 99582, Seattle, WA 98199, 1994.

Taylor, Carol. *Creative Bead Jewelry*. New York: Sterling Publishing Co., 1995.

Thompson, Angela. *Embroidery with Beads*. London: B.T. Batsford, 1987.

Wells, Carol Wilcox. *Creative Beadweaving*. Asheville, NC: Lark Books, 1996.

Videos

Blakelock, Virginia. *Bead Woven Necklaces*. Victorian Videos, POB 1540, Colfax, CA 95713.

Fowle, Kate. *Lampworked Beadmaking: Making Glass Beads*. Kate Fowle, 5420 Newark St., NW, Washington, DC 20016.

Hughes, Tory. *Mastering the New Clay I: Beginning Workshop, a Foundation Course in Polymer Clays* and 13 other polymer clay videos. Gameplan/Artranch, 2233 McKinley Ave., Berkeley, CA 94703.

Korach, Alice. *Bead Knitting with Alice Korach*. Victorian Videos, POB 1540, Colfax, CA 95713.

Perrenoud, Carol. *Beadweaving: Peyote Stitch*. Victorian Videos, POB 1540, Colfax, CA 95713.

ARTISTS' ADDRESSES

Chris Allen-Wickler
308 Prince St. #419
St Paul, MN 55101

Kenneth A. Arthur
4157 Hastings-
Newville Rd.
Lucas, OH 44843

Beth Barron
228 Xerxes Ave. North
Minneapolis, MN 55405

JoAnn Baumann
772 Grove St.
Glencoe, IL 60022

Terry Bell
9006 Gittins
Commerce Twp, MI
48382

Robert Burningham
1243 E. 4th St.
St. Paul, MN 55106

David Chatt
P.O. Box 113
Seattle, WA 98111

Olga Dvigoubsky
Cinnamon
1158 W. 23rd St.
Upland, CA 91784

Barb Davis
4684 15th St.
Wyandotte, MI 48192

Debra Dembowski
3212 S. 44th St.
Milwaukee, WI 53219

Sylvia deMurias
22 Cherry St.
Somerville, MA 02144

Rosie Dixon
28 W611 Berkshire Rd.
West Chicago, IL 60185

Joan Dulla
2961 S. Cholla
Chandler, AZ 85248

Nancy Eha
3898 Dellview Ave.
St. Paul, MN 55112

JoAnn Feher
1933 Broadway Ave.
East #1B
Seattle, WA 98102

Jacqui B. Fehl
12016½ Guerin St.
Studio City, CA 91604

Diane Fitzgerald
115 Hennepin Ave.
Minneapolis, MN 55401

Susan Etcoff Fraerman
1625 Freesia Circle
Highland Park, IL 60035

Jocelyn S. Giles
30 Forest Circle
Sedona, AZ 86336

Patty Haberman
826 W. Howe St.
Tempe, AZ 85281

Valorie Harlow
6490 Devonshire Dr.
Chanhassen, MN 55317

Kathryn Harris
2919 Granada Ave.
San Diego, CA 92104

Mimi Holmes
630 NE 4th St.
Minneapolis, MN 55413

John W. Lefelhocz
74 Second St.
Athens, OH 45701

Richard LeMieux
2183 Professor Ave. #4
Cleveland, OH 44113

Laura Leonard
2211 Pierce St. NE
Minneapolis, MN 55418

Lisa Lew
P.O. Box 4121
Whitefish, MT 59937

Eleanor Lux
P.O. Box 486
Eureka Springs, AR
72632

Liz Manfredini
19333 Palatine Ave. N
Seattle, WA 98133

NanC Meinhardt
1444 Toulon Ct.
Highland Park, IL 60035

Ann Terepaugh
Mitchell
28 Old Weston Rd.
Wayland, MA 01778

Nicole Nagel
P.O. Box 5308
Snowmass, CO 81615

Lisa Niforos
33 Pound Ave., #810
Brookline, MA 02146

Jan Nix-Westhoff
8805 Woodland Ave. E
Puyallup, WA 98371

Colleen O'Rourke
3656 N. Bosworth #2
Chicago, IL 60613

Amy Orr
415 S. 47th St.
Philadelphia, PA 19143

Kristen Frantzen Orr
1834 E. Inca Circle
Mesa, AZ 85208

Betty Pan
25 Montgomery Circle
New Rochelle, NY
10804

Christy Puetz
18249 Alamo St. NE
East Bethel, MN 55092

Madelyn C. Ricks
1520 Ohio Ave.
Lansing, MI 48906

Rachel Roggel
810 Goldenrod Ct.
Sunnyvale, CA 94086
(Jerusalem, Israel after
1999)

Ruth Marie Satterlee
5711 Phinney Ave.
North #102
Seattle, WA 98103

Pamela Schloff
5045 Abbott Ave. South
Minneapolis, MN 55410

Carol Shelton
P.O. Box 141379
Columbus, OH 43214

Nancy Smeltzer
9822 Pushcart Way
Columbia, MD 21045

Sandy Swirnoff
700 Douglas Ave. #909
Minneapolis, MN 55403

Thalia Tringo
19 Fairfield St.
Cambridge, MA 02140

Carolyn Veerjee
1719B Kenny Rd.
Columbus, OH 43212

Sally Wassink
555 Duboce Ave. #12
San Francisco, CA
94117

Dustin J. Wedekind
892 Michael Dr. #3
Campbell, CA 95008

Alison Whittemore
335 Army Blvd. #1
San Antonio, TX 78215

Michelle Williams
1416 Forest Ave.
Wilmette, IL 60091

Laura Willits
3401 NE 65th St. #201
Seattle, WA 98115